Our Mother and the

Shanghai YWCA in the 1930s

Autobiography of Helen Chung Teng

(鍾韶琴自傳)

By Henry S. Teng & Rosaline S. Teng Xu

鄧少林 鄧少笁 編輯

ISBN: 9798326913982

Publisher: Independently Published

Table of Contents

Preface

This book is based on the oral recordings of our mother, Mrs. Helen Chung Teng (English name: Helen Chung, Chinese name 鍾韶琴). After being meticulously compiled and edited, this book takes the form of a self-narrative autobiography. The book reflects mother's work as an industrial secretary at the Shanghai Young Women Christian Association (YWCA) and her significant contributions to the flourishing development of women's night schools in Shanghai, China during the 1930s.

Figure 1 Helen Chung in her 20s in the late 1920s.

In the early 1930s, our mother, Ms. Helen Chung, was one of the first industrial secretaries to reside in the ghetto area of Shanghai for textile workers in the western part of the city served by the Shanghai YWCA. Despite numerous challenges, she immersed herself in the harsh working and living conditions of female primarily textile factory workers, conducting home visits. By successfully integrating the process of teaching literacy and reading among female workers with their work and daily lives, she achieved remarkable results. This innovative teaching method, which combined practical social experiences, broke away from traditional educational models prevalent in church schools at the time. It left a profound impact and made significant contributions to the learning of basic reading and writing skills in Chinese and the awakening of minds of Shanghai's female worker community during that era. Even decades later, in the 1980s, her students still expressed heartfelt gratitude towards our mother in letters and photos.

In June 1980, an American graduate student named Emily Honig[1], a Ph.D. candidate from Stanford University, who was studying in China, visited our residence at Apartment unit 301, Building 6, Peking University. She was researching the Shanghai YWCA and women's night schools during the 1930s. Through introduction of others, Dr. Honig connected with our mother, Helen Chung, and engaged in an interview lasting nearly two

6

hours. During this meeting, she learned about the Shanghai YWCA women's night schools, textile workers of very young ages, and recorded the interview and our discussion.

At the time, the author, Henry Teng (or 鄧少林), assisted with the translation and recorded the conversation on his own tape recorder. Despite the migration to the United States and significant changes in life over the next four decades, this recording has been preserved until now. The content related to the Shanghai YWCA provided by our mother during that interview became the central theme of this book.

Our mother was born in 1904 in Fujian. Although official documents such as her Chinese passport, household registration, and U.S. immigration certificate state her birth year as 1910, she was actually born in 1904. Our grandfather, Zhong Chunhui (锺春晖)[2] worked as a Salt Duty Officer and was stationed in various places, including Dali (大理) in Yunnan(云南). As such, the family moved around a lot including our mother. Consequently, she entered schools relatively late and had to adjust her birthdate to facilitate enrollment.

Upon returning to China in 1956, mother filled out a registration form for the returning overseas students issued by the Foreign Experts Bureau of the Chinese State Council (中國國務院外國专家局, details can be found in her own handwriting in the appendix at the end of the book). The form indicates that father, Yen-lin Teng (鄧衍林 or Deng Yan-lin), mother and us, the kids, traveled together to China. We arrived in Shenzhen via a cruise ship named Wilson of the American President Line (APL), crossing the Pacific Ocean for twenty-one days on October 31, 1956. The reasons for returning to China listed by mother were: to serve the country; visit relatives (in Fuzhou); and provide higher education for the children. Mother's educational background was at the university graduate school level. After returning to China, her desired work included work related to the well-being of women, and the library (children's and reading departments), with expertise in adult education and library science.

Figure 2 Mother Helen Chung and father Prof. Yen-lin Teng in New York City in 1946.

Figure 3 Mother Helen Chung and father Prof. Yen-lin Teng in Beijing, China in the mid-1960s.

Mother listed the following credentials in her scholar registration form:

- **Passport**: Document No. 11234, issued on August 29, 1956, in Taiwan.

- **Educational Credentials**: Master's Degree in Education from Teachers College, Columbia University, New York (1946).

- **Service Credentials**: Certificate of service from the United Nations in New York, and a certificate from the New York City Public Library.

She listed her work experience as:

- **1927-1931**: Graduated from the Department of Sociology at Shanghai Hujiang University （上海滬江大學）

- **1931-1938 (August)**: Worked as an industrial secretary at the Shanghai Young Women Christian Association (YWCA) for eight years.

- **1935**: Conducted a social studies trip to Moscow and later attended a World YWCA conference in New York.

- **1938 (September)-1945 (July)**: Served as the General Secretary of the Kunming YWCA, China for seven years.

- **1945 (August)**: Attended World YWCA conference the second time in New York.

- **1945 (September)-1946 (June)**: Studied at Teachers College, Columbia University, New York, U.S.A.

- **1946 (October)-1950 (December)**: Worked as a liaison officer/director for the International Organizations at the United Nations Department of Public Information (DPI) in New

York.

- **1951 (January)-1954**: Managed household chores.

- **1955 (February)-1956 (September)**: Worked in the Children's Department of the Queens, New York Public Library.

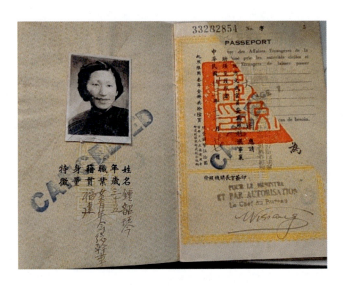

Figure 4 Mother Helen Chung's passport when returning to Mainland China in October 1956.

Figure 5 Father Prof. Yen-lin Teng's passport when returning to Mainland China in October 1956.

Figure 6 Mother Helen Chung Teng and father Prof. Yen-lin Teng in the United States of America during the 1950s.

After returning to China, mother faced challenges in finding work that aligned with her credentials and qualifications. She searched for positions related to sociology, adult education, and women's education based on her experience in Shanghai in the 1930s via the Foreign Experts Bureau of the Chinese State Council. Additionally, she explored opportunities similar to non-profit fundraising in Kunming and international liaison work akin to the United Nations. Given the conditions at the time, it was indeed a difficult task. Instead, mother focused her time and energy on educating and nurturing us, the children. It's worth noting that when we first returned, we, the kids, were like "foreigners," barely able to speak a word of Chinese, but were fluent in English. It was only a few years later that mother found employment at the Beijing National Library (北京圖書館).

Figure 7 A family group photo with grandma Ms. Xue Pei-ying in the center (薛 佩英) in 1961。Back row from left to right: author Henry S. Teng (鄧少林), brother Deng Yun-sheng(鄧云生), sister/author Rosaline S. Teng (鄧少釣).

Throughout her life, mother was deeply concerned about national and global affairs. During the period of the Anti-Japanese War, she joined the China Democratic League (中國民 主同盟) in Kunming and became an early member of the league. I remember her mentioning that Mr. Li Gongpu (李公樸), a leader of the Democratic League, introduced her to the organization. According to the *"Biography Dictionary of Famous Women from Ancient to Modern Times"* (古今中外女名人辭典) and official Committee communications, she served as a member of CPPCC National Committee(全國政協)[3] and the Central Liaison Working Committee of the Democratic League (中國民主同盟中央

聯絡工作委員會委員)[4].

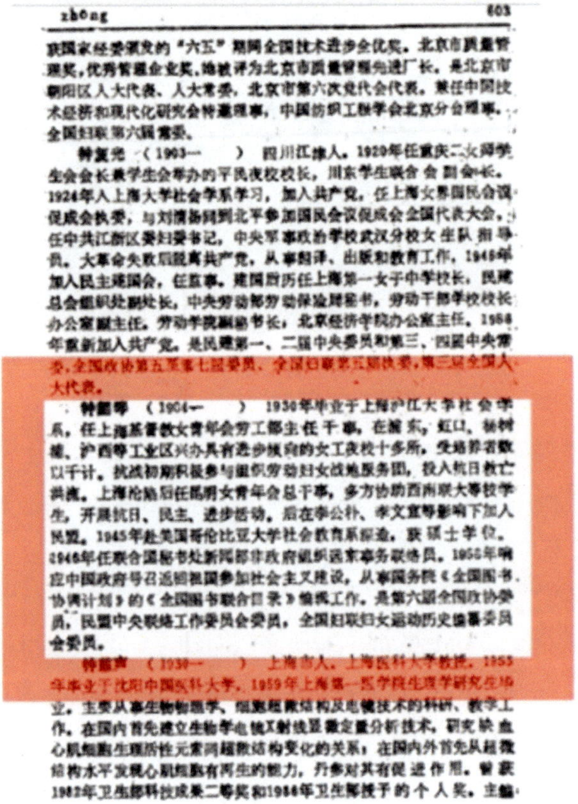

zhong 603

获国家经委颁发的"六五"期间全国技术进步全优奖、北京市质量管理奖，优秀管理企业奖，她被评为北京市质量管理先进厂长。是北京市朝阳区人大代表、人大常委，北京市第六次党代会代表。兼任中国技术经济和现代化研究会特邀理事，中国纺织工程学会北京分会理事，全国妇联第六届常委。

钟复光（1903— ）四川江津人。1920年任重庆二女师学生会会长兼学生会举办的平民夜校校长，川东学生联合会副会长。1924年入上海大学社会学系学习，加入共产党。任上海女界国民会议促成会执委，与刘清扬同到北平参加国民会议促成会全国代表大会。任中共江浙区委妇委书记，中央军事政治学校武汉分校女生队指导员。大革命失败后脱离共产党，从事翻译、出版和教育工作。1945年加入民主建国会，任监事。建国后历任上海第一女子中学校长，民建总会组织处副处长，中央劳动部劳动保险局秘书，劳动干部学校校长办公室副主任，劳动学院副秘书长，北京经济学院办公室主任。1984年重新加入共产党。是民建第一、二届中央委员和第三、四届中央常委，全国政协第五至第七届委员，全国妇联第三届执委，第三届全国人大代表。

钟韶琴（1904— ）1930年毕业于上海沪江大学社会学系。任上海基督教女青年会劳工部主任干事。在沪东、虹口、杨树浦、沪西等工业区兴办具有进步倾向的女工夜校十多所，受培养者数以千计。抗战初期积极参与组织劳动妇女战地服务团，投入抗日救亡洪流。上海沦陷后任昆明女青年会总干事，多方协助西南联大等校学生，开展抗日、民主、进步活动。后在李公朴、李文宜等影响下加入民盟。1945年赴美国哥伦比亚大学社会教育系深造，获硕士学位。1946年任联合国秘书处新闻部非政府组织远东事务联络员。1956年响应中国政府号召返回祖国参加社会主义建设，从事国务院《全国图书协调计划》的《全国图书联合目录》编纂工作。是第六届全国政协委员，民盟中央联络工作委员会委员，全国妇联妇女运动历史编纂委员会委员。

钟韶声（1930— ）上海市人。上海医科大学教授。1955年毕业于沈阳中国医科大学，1959年上海第一医学院生理学研究生毕业。主要从事生物物理学、细胞超微结构及电镜技术的科研、教学工作。在国内首先建立生物学电镜X射线显微定量分析技术，研究缺血心肌细胞生理活性元素同超微结构变化的关系；在国内外首先从超微结构水平发现心肌细胞有再生的能力，并参对其有促进作用。曾获1982年卫生部科技成果二等奖和1986年卫生部授予的个人奖。主编

Figure 8 Brief description of mother Helen Chung's biography in the "Biography Dictionary of Famous Women from Ancient to Modern Times" (古今中外女名人辭典) published in China.

In the article "*Enlightenment and Awakening of Chinese Women in the First Half of the 20th Century* (20 世纪上半叶中國妇女的启蒙

與觉醒)"[5], author Zhao Xiaoyang (趙曉陽) highly praised the work of industrial secretaries from the Shanghai YWCA during the 1930s. She stated, 'As Chinese women who were among the earliest to come into contact with Western society and thoughts, these Chinese and foreign YWCA industrial secretaries led China's female laborers. They bore witness to the multifaceted identities of being Chinese, female, and Christian. The relationship between Chinese women and Christianity should be evaluated and assessed against the backdrop of broader social and political changes in modern China.'

Prof. Elizabeth A. Littell-Lamb[6], an American historian specializing in women's movements and non-Western history, referred to the industrial secretaries from the Shanghai YWCA as 'Christian socialists' in one of her papers.

In 1987, mother immigrated to the United States and subsequently lived with both of our families, enjoying her senior years with her children and grandchildren. She passed away in California in November 2003. Her ashes were brought back to Beijing, China in 2005 to be interred alongside our father at the Beijing Babaoshan Cemetery (北京八寶山公墓).

Figure 9 First row from left to right: Jason Xu (grandson), Rosaline Teng Xu (daughter), mother Helen Chung Teng, Priscilla Liu (Joan's mother), Joan Teng (daughter-in-law). Second row from left to right: Wei-zhong Xu (son-in-law), Henry Teng (son).

2024 marks the 120th anniversary of our mother's, Mrs. Helen Chung Teng (鍾韶琴), birth year. We wholeheartedly dedicate this book to our beloved mother and father, as a testament to our enduring remembrance and deep affection for them.

Henry Shao-lin Teng (鄧少林)
and
Rosaline Shao-yun Teng Xu (鄧少筠)

United States and China, May 20, 2024

Serving the Shanghai YWCA from 1931 to 1938 by Helen Chung

Prelude by Henry S. Teng

According to the introduction in the article "The Christian Church and Labor Issues"[7] by author Zhao Xiaoyang, the Chinese Young Women's Christian Association (YWCA) has a history of over a hundred years. It is a religious organization that serves society with the spirit of Christ. In 1890, missionary John Leighton Stuart's mother and Frank Wilson Price's mother organized the first school-based YWCA for women in Hangzhou, China. In 1899, during the second national conference of the Chinese Young Men's Christian Association (YMCA) held in Shanghai, a preparatory committee for the Chinese YWCA was designated, consisting of both Chinese and Western women. That same year, the National Committee of the YWCA was established in Shanghai, responsible for external communication and expansion. In 1900, Annie Reynolds, the General Secretary of the World YWCA (serving from 1894 to 1904), visited China. The National Committee of the YWCA made contributions to the 25,000 female textile workers and 10,000 female match factory workers in Shanghai. They submitted a petition signed by 200 Shanghai female workers, urging the World YWCA to pay attention to women's labor issues in China.

Against this historical backdrop, my mother, Helen Chung Teng (鍾韶琴), began her studies at the Department of Sociology at Shanghai Hujiang University in 1927. She got involved with the Shanghai YWCA and embarked on a career there after graduating from college. This chapter captures my mother's self-recorded account of her work at the Shanghai YWCA's night school for female workers in the early 1930s. The content has been edited and compiled by the main editor, Henry S. Teng (鄧少林), based on a recorded speech during a conversation with my mother and an American graduate student in June 1980. The article aims to preserve my mother's speaking style and thought process.

Figure 10 Passport photo of Helen Chung on December 27, 1934.

Mother had previously published an article titled "The Lives of Female Workers as I Have Seen" in the May 1933 issue of the *Women's Youth Magazine* (Volume 12, Issue 5, page 46)[8].

Regarding the discourse on the Shanghai Young Women's Christian Association (YWCA) and the night school female workers during the 1930s, Elizabeth A. Littell-Lamb[9], a non-Western historian from the University of Tampa, Florida, wrote a scholarly paper. The title of her paper is "Engendering a Class Revolution: The Chinese YWCA Industrial Reform Work in Shanghai, 1927–1939"[10]. This paper specifically covers the period when your mother worked at the Shanghai YWCA, from 1931 to 1938.

The article cites numerous documents, including work reports from both American and Chinese YWCA officials who collaborated with your mother. Notable figures mentioned include May Bagwell, Lily Haass, and Mrs. Deng Yuzhi.

According to Professor Littell-Lamb's abstract: "Starting in 1927 Young Women's Christian Association (YWCA) industrial secretaries made creating a literate working-class leadership for a female labor movement their primary goal. When the Association's conservative middle-class National Committee refused to approve that goal, they pursued it by establishing night schools for factory women. They taught factory women to read and write while also introducing them to socialist ideas of workers' organization and feminist ideas of women's empowerment. Industrial secretaries carried out a 'class revolution' within the Association, breaking down the Association's class barriers by insisting the Chinese YWCA include women of all socio-economic classes. The result was a modicum of success in training leaders for a women's labor movement and, at least in policy, the inclusion of working women as full-fledged YWCA members".

In our own research for this book, while going over archives of the World YWCA and its associations in China maintained by Smith College[11], we found the following valuable artifacts titled "(Shanghai YWCA) A Few Facts about the Industrial Department and its Work - Program of Education on Industrial and Economic Questions within the Association and in the Community"[12] from the Shanghai YWCA documentation bin. The artifacts also included a pamphlet with a Chinese title of "上海女青年會勞工部工作之一班"[13].

INDUSTRIAL DEPARTMENT
SHANGHAI: Y. W. C. A.
OFFICE: 302 NANKING ROAD
TELEPHONE 64495

CHAIRMAN INDUSTRIAL COMMITTEE:—
   MISS YANG AI-FANG
SECRETARIES · · MISS CHUNG SHOU-CHING
   MISS LIU YU-YING
   MISS MAY BAGWELL

A FEW FACTS ABOUT THE INDUSTRIAL DEPARTMENT AND ITS WORK

Program of Education on Industrial and Economic Questions Within the Association and in the Community

The Industrial Committee which is composed of women of varied interests is undertaking not only to study and try to meet the needs of women workers but to try to stimulate public interest in industrial conditions affecting women workers so that there may be developed in the community a sense of responsibility for working to raise the standards under which they work and live.

Program with Women Workers

WESTERN DISTRICT INDUSTRIAL CENTRE—131 San Ho Li, Ferry Rd. & 4488 Yu Ching Li, Robinson Rd.
A centre for experiment, demonstration and training of secretaries, under the direction of the Industrial Departments of the National Y. W. C. A. and Shanghai Y. W. C. A.

Program:

Educational Work—
  Classes—
    Popular Education—under the supervision of the Association Popular Education Secretary.
    Arithmetic, hygiene letter writing, Chinese History & Geography, etc., for graduates of Popular Education classes.
  Group Work—
    Club work, based on interests and needs of women workers.
    Clubs are represented in the Joint Representative Group which brings together members of all the industrial clubs and meets monthly at the Y.W.C.A. headquarters.
    Special groups for married women workers.
  Mass education with larger groups of workers and their families.
  Library service, making available books and other reading material which can be read by graduates of Popular Education classes.
  Health Education—Emphasis on personal health, public health and health in the home thru talks, discussions, demonstration, movies etc.
  Dr. Z. T. Wong is giving her services two evenings a month for making physical examinations and giving medical advice to women workers.
  Home Visiting by teachers and secretary.

A Hostel for Women Workers—a small hostel which serves as a demonstration in homemaking and furnishes clean comfortable living quarters for nine girls who have no family near enough to live with.

Leisure Time Activities—club rooms open during time workers are free from work and during times of unemployment for reading, music, games and other forms of recreation.

OTHER CENTRES WHERE DEPARTMENT CARRIES ON WORK—
In Yangste Poo, Pootung and Hongkow Districts rooms are rented or loaned by other organizations and work is carried on which is of a similar nature to that in the Western District Centre but more limited as the staff in the Western District Centre live in the centre.

NUMBER OF REGULAR MEMBERS NOW BEING REACHED:

Organized Clubs	...	...	...	...	...	...	...	...	150
Classes	...	...	...	...	...	...	...	...	800
ATTENDANCE DURING SEPTEMBER AND OCTOBER ...		...	...	...	...	...		...	1368

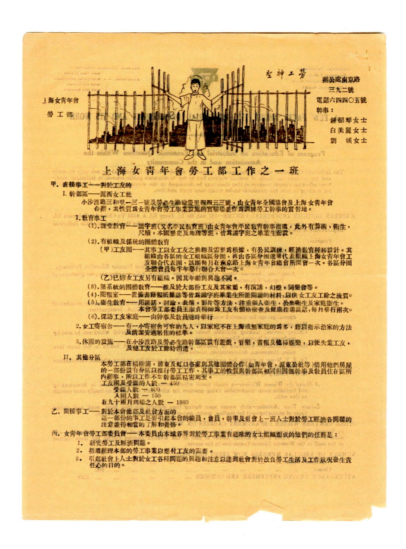

The artifacts showed a Shanghai YWCA guiding education program / pamphlet both in English and Chinese that bears our mother's name (Chung Shou-ching or 鍾韶琴) and the industrial secretary team that she worked with. Further research is required to understand the significance of this document and

26

many other artifacts in the Sophia Smith Collection of Women's History.

Majoring in Sociology (Manufacturing Labor) at the Shanghai Hujiang University (上海滬江大學)

At that time, I was studying in Fuzhou City, Fujian Province, China. While studying, we had summer vacations every summer. The Shanghai YWCA had a student department and organized student summer camps in the summer. At that time, I participated in the student summer camp organized by the YWCA during my student days. I participated once or twice[14].

Figure 11 Helen Chung (鍾韶琴) in her 20s in the late 1920s.

Later, I gradually became interested in YWCA and participated in some activities. I gained a lot and made many friends. At that time, I began to feel that the YWCA was very meaningful. Therefore, I became interested in the YWCA at that time. After I graduated from middle school, I went to Hong Kong to study. I graduated from junior high school in Fuzhou and went to Hong Kong to study high school after junior high school graduation. After finishing high school, I studied at the University of Hong Kong for a year. Later, because my father worked in salt affairs and often changed jobs, he originally worked in Beihai, Guangdong Province.

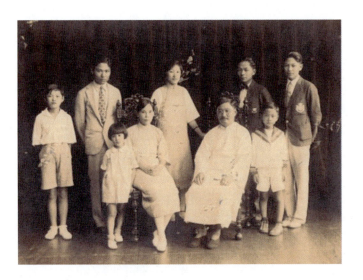

Figure 12 Family photo. Helen Chung in the middle of the second row. Her father, Zhong Chun-hui (鍾春暉), first row second from the right, mother Xue Pei-ying (薛佩英), first row second from the left.

He was from the Salt Affairs Bureau, which is like customs and collects taxes. At that time, the Salt Affairs Bureau, Customs and Post Office seemed to be repaying foreign debts. At that time, taxes were used to repay debts at that time. He worked there. This job changed every two or three years, so my father originally worked in salt affairs in Yunnan and then was transferred to Beihai, Guangdong Province. Beihai, Guangdong Province is close to Hong Kong, so after finishing my studies in Fuzhou, I went to Hong Kong to study. After studying there, I transferred from the University of Hong Kong to Shanghai Hujiang University (上海滬江大學) in Shanghai. This was in 1927. In 1927 I studied at a university in Shanghai and graduated from the Shanghai Hujiang University in 1930[15]. My major at Hujiang was sociology (major). At that time Deng Zhongxia was not at Hujiang University and it may have been later. Chen Zhengya was my mentor and he was the head of the sociology department. My major (major) was sociology and my minor (minor) was education. Therefore, in my graduation thesis I did a small thesis on the life of female workers. Because Hujiang University had set up a night school in Yangshupu at that time and Hujiang University also set up a night school at that time. They were mainly male workers with some female workers and education was for ordinary people to teach them literacy education. Later on, I did some survey work through their school to understand the life of female workers and then I had some understanding of the life of female workers from here on out. I also liked it very much and was willing to do this work. When I graduated, the personnel department of the YWCA sent staff every year to various universities to introduce the work of the YWCA. There were student departments, dormitory departments, member departments, girl departments and labor departments which introduced the work of the YWCA comprehensively to see which aspect of work you were interested in. Later on, when I heard about the Labor Department, I became interested in it. At that time if someone was interested then the YWCA would talk to them carefully again later on. Later on, I talked with Ms. Lili Huss[16] who was an American and there were many American staff members at the YWCA at that time. So, she introduced me to the YWCA and I felt interested and liked it very much and expressed my willingness to do it. Later on, after several trials when I officially graduated, I started working at the YWCA.

Working for the Shanghai YWCA

When I came to the YWCA[17], it happened that the YWCA had a staff member, also an American staff member named Ms. May Bagwell[18] (白美麗)[19], who worked with me and led me in my work. At that time when I first arrived, I didn't know much about how to do the work. She worked with me. Ms. Bai Meili was more progressive and very humble and I worked very well with her. The Shanghai YWCA is of course a local city YWCA and there is also a national YWCA above it, such as Deng Yuzhi (Cora Deng) [20] and others. We are considered a local YWCA. The YWCA can also be said to be international because there is a world YWCA organization. Each country has a YWCA and there is also a world YWCA organization. So, speaking of it, this is an international women's organization with religious characteristics as well. Although it has religious characteristics, it is different from the church because we do not preach but serve in the spirit of Christ. This is why the YWCA hangs a sign called the Christian YWCA. We do not preach or require that one be a believer. This is different from the church. Speaking of it, the YWCA is international and of course has religious characteristics but we do not preach. Our service targets are women, housewives, students, girls, female workers and rural women. Our labor department specializes in working with female workers. When I went there in 1930[21] there were already three schools. This labor department opened female worker night schools in several large industrial areas to give female workers the opportunity to study. Because at that time most workers were illiterate and very few could read or write. Of course, our main goal was to give them some cultural level and gradually raise their awareness. We started by saying that if female workers have problems let them solve them themselves. When I went there it was like this, solve it yourself. If you want to solve it yourself you need to have culture first and after you have culture you need to have training so that they have their own independent ability to handle their own labor issues. At that time, we had some problems which were slowly changed due to the influence of social trends and progressive trends as well as the work of the Communist Party on the periphery which had contact with us and our work also underwent many changes. At that time when I went there were three female worker night schools one in Pudong one in Yangshupu and one in Zhaofeng Road because these places were all in large industrial areas. Among these night schools according to some materials I saw Pudong night school started in 1928 and was the earliest one followed by Yangshupu night school which I went to all three schools. Pudong was completely concentrated in cigarette factories where factories made cigarettes while Yangshupu Road was a textile industrial area while Zhaofeng Road also had many cigarette factories. Zhaofeng Road and Yangshupu because they were cigarette factories only had day shifts no night shifts with 12 hour day shifts after which female workers came to our female worker night school for classes from 7:00 pm to 9:00 pm for two hours after finishing work they quickly ate dinner and came to our school while Yangshupu had two shifts one in the morning and one at night because those who worked night shifts immediately came to our school after finishing work from 7:00 am to 9:00 am while those who worked day shifts came to school from 7:00 pm to 9:00 pm this is talking about the situation of the schools classes were like this each school had two teachers some had three teachers we staff members went there mainly to hire teachers and see how they taught classes besides this we also organized some activities for students which changed names several times when we first went it was called Citizen Association later this name was easily misunderstood by workers who didn't understand so it was changed to Workers Solidarity Association which means workers unite later on we felt this name was too obvious as if workers were organizing themselves making our work difficult to carry out with obstacles so we changed it to Shining Friends Association[22] so how did Shining Friends Association come about? Our YWCA had a girl department called Shining China Association so we changed it to Shining Friends Association everyone being friends uniting can emit light meaning shining this name was more suitable everyone felt this name was more suitable easier to understand some who were originally afraid and unwilling now willing to participate our organization outside of class was like this meeting once a week talking about current events singing sometimes even acting starting out using this for propaganda work later on many works were done through this organization.

Living and Working in the Ghettos of Shanghainese Workers

Our organization outside of class was like this, meeting once a week to talk about current events, sing and sometimes even act. Starting out using this for propaganda work later on many works were done through this organization. Later on, when I went, I went with Ms. May Bagwell (白美麗 or Bai Meili) because Shanghai West Xiao Sha De Street[23] and Lao Bo Sheng Street had many factory workers and looked like a future industrial area that would develop so we went to that place to find a rented house. These night schools on Xiao Sha De Street, Zhao Fong Street and Pudong Yang Shu Pu were all borrowed from other people's places with Pudong Yang Shu Pu night school being borrowed by the YWCA early on. Zhao Fong Street night school was also borrowed from a middle school's classroom and was borrowed at night. Yangshupu night school was also borrowed. If Hujiang University had a place we would borrow their school's place to run it. Later on, we thought we should rent our own house and at that time there were many new houses and Deng Yuzhi also mentioned it so we found two houses in San He Li location that could be rented. The bottom layer was used as a classroom and the upstairs classroom was for teachers and staff to live in. We thought that in addition to teaching staff and teachers hoped to have more contact with workers and understand more about the situation it would be best to live in the worker area. Xiao Sha De Street and Lao Bo Sheng Street were surrounded by places where workers lived so we chose this place. We rented two houses on Xiao Sha De Street and May Bagwell and I lived there. In addition to the two of us there were also teachers living there.

At that time, the faculty was also introduced by the director, and there were people she knew, and there was no standard, I thought she had experience and could teach.

After the school started, I lived on Xiao Sha De Street, where Ms. Bai Meili also lived. A year or two later, Deng Yuzhi also lived there. Xiao Sha De Street was set up, and the area there was different from the rest. Because there are mainly textile mills, as well as silk mills, and also cigarettes, mainly textile mills. Their factories have night shifts and day shifts, so our school has classes during the day and classes at night. A year later, the school grew so fast that the school could no longer accommodate it. Rented 2 more houses on Lao Bo Sheng Street and started night classes. Many female workers come from the countryside and they don't have a place to live, so we set up a dormitory for women workers upstairs so that they can live in it and the teachers can live there. Downstairs as classrooms, so that two schools were opened, and later there were more factories, and there was a school in Cao Jia Du. This resulted in a total of six schools. After a few years, we had graduating students.

Because we have limited finances, they run their own schools, we YWCA provide books, and they get money from somewhere else. The nature of the school they run is the same as ours. In this way, we developed a total of 10 schools, four of them female workers, and we had six. In the beginning, there were not many students, only one or two. It later grew to more than 1,000 people. We are held quarterly, a total of 2 quarters. Regarding the work, we have carried out a very good job, mainly for them to learn the Chinese language, mainly literacy (for reading and writing). We believe that after addressing the literacy problem, they should be able to do everything themselves. In addition to the above courses, our textbooks are language, but also mathematics. At first, they were very simple textbooks, but later the textbooks could not meet our needs, so we made up our own. The content is a little deeper. The content is compiled by someone, there is political content, there is society, and there is political and economic common sense. There is also the trade union movement, the women's movement. We used to have a set of these textbooks, but now we can't find them. The content of the textbook is mainly written by people. But it is still up to the instructors, who can speak from the textbooks and play their own content, all in simple terms, and related to the lives of female workers. For example, there is a lesson about people, workers are people, but why do they live so hard. Later, it was slowly introduced that workers were exploited by capitalists and so on. "Workers are humans but our life is hard (工人是人，生活苦)", these seven characters though simple, meant a lot to them. This is just an example. This is our course situation.

Training the "Trainers" from Women Workers

Regarding the school, we are divided into 3 levels: beginner, intermediate and advanced classes. It takes a total of 3 years. After graduation, it is equivalent to graduating from elementary school. Later, as we had more years and more graduates, we felt that these students could continue to be trained, so we added a special class. The special class is specifically for training students to become junior teachers[24]. The elementary school system can train teachers. We hire them from the special class students to be teachers in the school. At that time, they were off the job. They no longer went to the factory and taught full-time. Our sources of teachers were graduates from our school and friends we knew who were introduced to us. Later, the quality of the teachers was better and more progressive. These friends included Mr. Tao Xingzhi. Mr. Tao Xingzhi was in Shanghai. He knew many progressive teachers in popular education. There were those introduced by Mr. Tao Xingzhi and those introduced by the Communist Party. We didn't know the details of these people.

We knew friends who came to be teachers, and later they introduced other teachers. Gradually the quality of our teachers changed and they were all relatively progressive. That's the situation with the teachers. In addition to extracurricular activities, there was a lot of mobility among students coming to class. Why was there so much mobility? Because they had to work 12 hours a day regardless of wind or rain. They had to come to class even after working night shifts. I felt very sad when I saw them because their eyes couldn't even open. Of course, sometimes there were household chores and they couldn't come. Some were sick, some were opposed by their families and couldn't come to class, etc., so there were quite a few absences.

Visiting the Women Workers in Their Homes

In addition to teaching, our teachers had another major task: visiting students' homes. We felt this work was very important. Not only did the teachers visit the homes, but I also visited the homes. If a student didn't come for 12 days, we would go see if she was sick or if there was a problem at home or at the factory. We would go see them and get close to them in this way. In this way, if a student had a problem, she would come to where we lived, near Sanhe Li[25]. We had many students coming to us every day. If they couldn't come, we would go to their homes. The teachers taught from 7:00 to 9:00 pm, so during the day, in addition to preparing lessons, they would go see the students. At first when we went on home visits, their families were a little scared. Later when we went, they were not afraid because we told them that we were mainly concerned about them not coming to class and also asked if they had any difficulties in life. So, their problems might be family disputes or illness or financial difficulties etc. When the female workers were sick, we had a special organization at that time to help establish a Social Work Case. These cases were managed by a special person. Case problems included financial difficulties, illness or other problems such as marriage issues etc. Our social worker or case worker would specifically visit these female workers and record these situations. If they needed financial help for medical treatment, we would ask a doctor. This doctor was specifically for treating our female workers.

When female workers were sick, they would specifically go to see this doctor. There was a Labor Affairs Committee Member who was also a doctor. If it didn't work out, they would be referred to a hospital. I remember I had several students who had tuberculosis, lymphatic tuberculosis and intestinal tuberculosis etc. There were also other minor illnesses and we would refer them to our doctor. When they recovered from their illness, they could come back to class. Some had marriage problems and we would introduce them to a lawyer to help them solve their problems. If they shouldn't divorce, we would persuade them to reconcile. If some problems should be divorced and they really couldn't get along, we would help. Our home visit work was well done and later there were fewer student absences. Later on, the students gradually understood us. At first, they didn't understand and thought where there could be such a good thing as going to school for free and they were suspicious.

We recruited students twice a year. After posting the notice, many students saw it and came. At first, they were a little suspicious, but later on they gradually understood and our work became easier. The second method was that after they benefited, they went out to propagate and many students were brought in by them. This is the development of our school.

For our way of working, in addition to classroom education, there are visits and solving individual problems. There were also many social education issues, such as at that time there was a Bureau of Industries with labor laws. We also let female workers know through this Bureau of Industries that labor laws are good and that factories should have certain guarantees. This labor law was well spoken but not implemented in the Bureau of Industries. If we found any problems in the factory, we would also write letters jointly with the students to report to the Bureau of Industries which factories were illegal. Later on, when we wrote letters, some were effective and some were ineffective. Through these we also educated them to realize that it was not feasible. Especially to let them know that if it is not feasible, they need to liberate themselves. This is our educational process and purpose.

Joining the Anti-Japanese Movements

After the September 18th Incident, their work shifted to anti-Japanese salvation work. At that time, they promoted anti-Japanese salvation. Their patriotic songs were not allowed to be sung, so they turned the songs into dramas and sang them through these dramas. They used speeches to promote this work and promote anti-war salvation. Of course, this work was not done by them alone. Because at that time they went through teachers and many progressive people, through the progressive writers they knew, and there were also directors in the drama. They invited them to help. At the beginning, their students wrote their own scripts. After writing, they performed their own plays. They felt that the level of the script was not enough, so they asked outsiders to help improve it. Singing was the same, and they also asked people outside to help. Especially at graduation ceremonies, they also took the opportunity to conduct propaganda. There were singing meetings and dramas. This form was very good. The plays performed by female workers' students were very touching and they all sang by themselves. In addition to their students, they also brought people from other factories and brought their friends to watch the play and brought friends from the factory to watch the play.

Sometimes their auditorium was not big enough, so they went to the large auditorium of the Women's Youth Association or used the school auditorium. Students came and people from other factories who knew each other came to participate in graduation ceremonies. There were also May Day and March 8th Women's Day commemorations. They took this opportunity to hold a large meeting. In addition to their own students performing dramas, singing, dancing, they also invited progressive people in society to give speeches and speeches. This was also a very good method. In addition to this activity, they privately contacted many students. Sometimes when students came to talk to them, they could take this opportunity to talk deeper and they were willing to do so. The most common topic of conversation was about work and the working conditions in the factory. Their work was quite bitter and quite tiring. They worked for twelve hours a day and only got 8 yuan, 12 yuan or a maximum of 16 yuan a day. The factories they saw there were the most bitter silk factories where silk was drawn. When they went to see it, there were all child laborers in the factory. And their hands were soaked in water all day long and their hands were rotten. That was the hardest part. They were all child laborers who were eleven or twelve years old or around ten years old[26] when they spoke up. There was also a spinning mill at that time when they went in and there was cotton in the air. Not only was the environment bad but it was also abused. Usually there were foremen oppressing them. Later when they went to class and talked with them, they united together. The money they earned was not enough they were all from rural areas and had to send money back home leaving little money for themselves These things were often talked about by them They were from rural areas but very few returned to rural areas

Because comparatively speaking although it was relatively bitter in the factory it was even more bitter in rural areas Still staying in the factory So sometimes work was not good you could change workshops but it was very difficult to transfer work Generally still staying in the original place Until they got married had children got sick then left They could do it just kept doing it To maintain their own lives Of course those of them who had read books had some knowledge did propaganda work inside encouraged everyone to unite together helped solve problems in their hard work.

Because there was no culture at that time, they believed in fate and endured it as it was brought by fate. Later, as they gradually read books and realized that this was not brought by fate, but was related to the social system. We could see that they gradually understood and indeed made progress. Later, after 3 years, their propaganda speeches and artistic performance abilities were all pretty good. And they came out to work when they were young. To think about it, they had already worked for 12 hours a day and then came to class. If I were asked to do it, I couldn't do it. It was really too tiring and they just closed their eyes. But their spirits were very good. They gradually became more sensible later. Whether they read books or not was related to their poverty. So, when they started reading books, they were more motivated and capable. And our work could not be separated from the influence of the Communist Party. At that time, we didn't know because the Communist Party was underground. However, we could see the signs even though they were still working underground.

As for the development direction of our work, we also followed the trend and influence of progress at the beginning, and gradually understood a little bit by ourselves. Like when I first went there, I didn't understand it very well and I wasn't clear about it. Ms. Bagwell had worked in the United States and knew more about female worker education. There was also Deng Yuzhi who helped us and gave us guidance. There were also many progressive people helping. Later our teachers not only taught but also made home visits. We held a teacher meeting every month to exchange experiences, raise teaching issues, discuss how to improve and improve textbooks. After the meeting we could clearly improve.

The school's large-scale meeting must be held once. We have it every year or every 2 years or every 3 years. We also organized a study meeting which was a teacher study meeting which lasted for several days. We invited some people outside to give lectures. The meeting place was at the Women's Youth Association headquarters. On the student side we later developed to host summer camps or summer meetings which was in 1937 before the outbreak of the Anti-Japanese War in the summer. We held a summer meeting in South Asia in Shanghai which was completely composed of students elected from the Shining Friends Club with more than 40 people. At that time we knew that the day of anti-war was coming In addition to discussing practical matters there were also some speeches We also talked about first aid training students organizing training classes I remember that what we mainly discussed was what is capitalism (system) and socialism (system) mentioned So what is capitalism like and what is socialism like We didn't say it clearly After the meeting we just talked casually about two roads to choose from It's clear at a glance It's placed there We can't go this way We started with democracy Because the Women's Youth Association has a board of directors Underneath the board of directors is the labor department The labor department also organizes a labor committee In addition to being interested in labor this labor committee also invites our teachers and students to participate We think this is a democratic form Female workers' students can raise questions at the meeting and then raise them to the board of directors As a result this path gradually became impassable because female workers had to take leave They had no rest days Students had to take leave frequently which didn't work They had speaking rights there but how much could be implemented I don't know

These are some experiments that don't work There are also factory laws and other provisions that cannot be realized From here they learned lessons got education couldn't go through so they had to come by themselves and take the revolutionary road.

In our anti-war year we held summer camps or summer meetings The August 13th incident came Our Women's Youth Association temporarily suspended women's activities The factory also stopped Students couldn't go to class anymore Later many refugees came concentrated in Shanghai's concession which was relatively safe.

So, we started to do refugee work and organized students and teachers. Our refugee work started by doing something in the refugee camp, helping them with hygiene and helping with registration. The refugees were from rural areas, from bombed areas, and from areas occupied by the Japanese. Later these refugees all poured into the concession. Most of these refugees walked in and came into the concession. There were also those who came by car. At that time there were refugee shelters and there was an organization called something I can't remember. It was an anti-Japanese salvation organization. We all joined in. We also joined together to run this refugee shelter. Later our Women's Youth Association also ran a shelter for women and children refugees which specialized in sheltering women and children. Part of our strength was concentrated there. I organized the work there and at the same time there were teachers and students and we all worked together. There were married women in the shelter for women and children as well as unmarried women. There were single women and those with children. Their husbands did not come with them but were women and children. Some husbands went to other refugee shelters. When other shelters could not accommodate them, they sent women to us. Because there was not enough space for refugees, we organized a shelter specifically for women and children with women with children because the refugee shelter was too crowded to take care of the children Later, we opened another shelter for women children and women with children Organize the refugees. They cook their own meals. The children are also organized. They go to kindergarten, so that adults can do things. At the same time, they also organize literacy classes for them.

1937年10月5日上海劳动妇女战地服务团成立留影

从左至右：李慧英、李亚芬、龚琦伟、柳秀娟、秦秋谷、胡兰畦、胡瑞英、任秀棠、郑惠珍、张定堡、金敏玉

Figure 13 The All Shanghainese Working Women (Anti-Japanese) Medic Brigade was established on October 5, 1937. The Brigade was led by General Ms. Hu Lan-xi (holder of name flag). (Source of information: 浦东档案、浦东妇联, URL: https://www.sohu.com/a/451657698_120209938.)

Figure 14 The executive industrial secretaries of the Shanghai YWCA sent off their worker students to join the All Shanghainese Working Women (Anti-

Japanese) Medic Brigade on October 4, 1937. Helen Chung is in the middle of the third row. Ms. Deng Yu-zhi or Cora Deng (鄧裕志) is the first from the left in the third row. Ms. Zhang Shu-yi (張淑義) is the first from the right in the third row.

Some of our students participated in anti-Japanese activities by the end of 1937. They joined the All Shanghainese Working Women (Anti-Japanese) Medic Brigade (上海勞動婦女抗日戰地服務團)[27], which was a field service team composed of worker women led by Hu Lanxi (胡蘭畦)[28]. After the field service team contacted us[29], we told the students about it. The students were also willing to go. The first batch was ten people. After they went there, they followed the army and did service work in the army. They went there to do propaganda work, sing songs and perform plays. They also sewed clothes, did nursing work and helped wounded soldiers. After they went out, the effect was very good, so there were second and third batches and even fourth batches later to join the field service team. Later, it was not only laborers who participated, but also students. As I just said, we also have a part of female workers and students who worked as refugees and went to Shanghai Huajing Hospital. They went to work as nurses in hospitals where there were injured soldiers.

In 1938, I went to Kunming City in Yunnan Province to do things for the YWCA[30] there. Kunming was a big rear area at that time.

50

The work of the Shanghai Women's Youth Association was done by Zhang Shuyi (张淑义)[31]. The Women's Youth Association also started activities in Kunming and it was the same as in Shanghai. There were labor departments, student departments, membership departments, and girls' departments etc., and some dormitories were also set up.

So, I have heard some information about the Women's Youth Association before I went there, but there are no documents describing it. Our Shanghai Women's Youth Association just started activities and held women's classes in factories, which were literacy classes for female workers. It was set up in factories and held classes for some time before it failed. At that time, literacy classes were a bit evangelical and used the Bible and prayer. I heard them talking about it this way but there are no documents about this matter. This kind of class did not last long in factories because how could factories allow such things to happen? Because generally factories do not welcome this kind of literacy class thing. Going to factories to hold classes is always unsuccessful. After doing this for a while, the Women's Youth Association stopped. Of course, the Shanghai Women's Youth Association has a long history and when I went there it had been around for decades already. I went there in the 1930s. It was officially organized by the Women's Youth Association to run women's night schools in 1928.

(The descriptions above are based on a recording of Ms. Helen Chung's speech, recorded and edited by Henry S. Teng.)

Time is Like a Song – Helen Chung Autobiography (1904 – 1956) by Helen Chung

Prelude by Rosaline S. Teng Xu

This autobiography of my mother Helen Chung Teng (鍾韶琴) was written based on a recording and was shared with family members in 2003, just before we celebrated mother's 100th birthday in Foster City, California. The 100th came from a Chinese Lunar calendar tradition, where a child in China is born with age one (a person's age is always one year older on his/her birthday anniversary). There were articles written by others about the Shanghai YWCA and mother that I gathered and placed in a Souvenir Collection as a birthday gift to mother. The following is mother's autobiography based on her oral recordings.

My Grandparents

My grandparents were originally illiterate farmers from Gutian (古田), Fujian(福建). In the late 19th century, foreign missionaries established churches and conducted missionary activities around Fuzhou. At that time, the American Methodist Episcopal

Church deeply proliferated Gutian with Christianity. My grandparents started attending church and also enrolled in the school associated with the church, which transformed their cultural outlook and lives. My grandfather, a clever man, gradually became a pastor within the church. He even compiled a dictionary using the Romanization system, which provided phonetic annotations for Chinese characters in the Fuzhou dialect. This allowed people to understand how each character should be pronounced in Fuzhou dialect and vice versa, enabling them to look up its meanings. It's said that this dictionary was widely circulated in the southeastern region, and even in the 1970s, people from Singapore contacted us requesting copies.

My grandfather raised five sons and two daughters, ensuring they received a good education. Around 1915, when I returned to Fuzhou, my grandparents were already elderly and had moved from Gutian to live in Fuzhou. Later, my father used his savings to collaborate with my grandfather on constructing several houses in Fuzhou, which became known as "Ke Yuan(可園)." During their later years, my grandparents managed and operated these properties in Fuzhou.

My Life as a Teenager

As for my teenage years, I was born in Fuzhou. At that time, my father (鍾春暉 Or Zhong Chunhui) had graduated from Fujian Yinghua Academy and was working in Shanghai. Initially, he worked at the Translation Bureau, translating English into Chinese. I recall that he translated English versions of Russian literary works into Chinese for publication. Both his Chinese and English were commendable. My father was upright, meticulous, and reserved. He disliked socializing and never engaged in corrupt practices. Even at home, he rarely spoke.

Later, my mother (薛佩英 or Xue Peiying) and I joined my father in Shanghai, living not far from his workplace. Around 1900, the Boxer Rebellion ended, and the Qing government had paid astronomical reparations of 450 million taels of silver. Consequently, the Qing government's tax revenue was entirely mortgaged. Customs, salt duty administration, and postal services were major sources of revenue, all controlled by foreigners. The heads of these institutions were Westerners. Salt Duty administration was recruiting managers, and besides requiring a certain level of education, proficiency in English was crucial. Having a religious background made it easier for candidates to be hired. My father saw the favorable conditions in salt duty administration, including high income, and decided to take the exam. He was successful and became a salt duty administration officer. Initially, he worked near Shanghai, but after gaining familiarity with the job, he discovered that working in remote areas yielded significantly higher income. Many people were unwilling to go to these underdeveloped regions, but my father decided to give it a try. He left Shanghai and went to Kunming, specifically the Kunming Salt Duty Administration Bureau.

We lived in Kunming for a while, and our family grew with the addition of two younger brothers. As the children grew older, education became a significant concern. During the chaotic early years of the Republic of China, the mainland lacked schools compared to the coastal areas. We had to hire an elderly teacher who taught basic literacy and classical literacy.

Soon after, my father was transferred to the extremely backward and remote Muhei (雲南目黑古鎮、鹽都). I remember the 16-day journey, with me riding in a sedan chair, my two brothers sharing another chair, and my parents each in their own. My mother even held our youngest brother. Salt duty police officers with rifles accompanied us on both sides. At the time, bandits were rampant, so we could only travel during daylight hours. We finally arrived in Muhei Jing, where fortunately, my father's position allowed us to live in a good large house. I recall an incident when I was holding my youngest brother on the balcony railing upstairs. He squirmed, and my strength wasn't enough to hold him, causing him to fall from the balcony. I was terrified, but luckily, he cried briefly, and nothing serious happened.

The main issue remained education. We hired an old teacher who could only teach basic classical literacy. My mother supervised us, ensuring we memorized the material. By the time I was 14 or 15, I was still obedient and had learned well. However, my younger brothers were mischievous and didn't study seriously. This situation couldn't continue, so I was sent back to Fuzhou to be with my grandparents. I entered a church school and immediately joined junior high. Later, my younger brother also returned to Fuzhou, and we lived with our grandparents for several years.

After graduating from junior high school, my father was transferred to Beihai in Guangxi. Beihai is a port city, not far from Hong Kong, and there were regular ships connecting the two. My father knew a Korean man working at the customs, and his daughter attended St. Stephen's Girls' College in Hong Kong, which was reputed to be a good school. So, my father sent me and my younger brother to study there—me at the girls' school and him at the boys' school. This marked the beginning of our high school life. St. Stephen's College was well-known, and students who excelled there could directly enter the University of Hong Kong. At that time, getting into the University of Hong Kong was quite challenging. Somehow, I managed to pass the entrance exam and spent a year studying there. During this period, my father was transferred from Beihai to Wutongqiao, Sichuan, which was near Mount Emei. Consequently, I left the University of Hong Kong and enrolled in the sociology department at Shanghai Hujiang University.

Not long after, my father was transferred back to Yexian, which was not far from Shanghai but still quite remote. The house there was nice—a small Western-style building. This allowed my mother, younger siblings, and me to reunite. In the 1980s, my brother Ping-jiu came to visit us from Taiwan to see our mother, and we even went to Yexian near Shanghai to check if the house we used to live in was still there. Unfortunately, we couldn't find it. In 1931, I graduated from Hujiang University in Shanghai. During my university years, I wasn't particularly active. Coincidentally, the Young Women Christian Association (YWCA) visited the university every year to recruit staff. Given my background in sociology and family ties to religion, I applied and became a YWCA industrial secretary in Shanghai, earning a monthly salary of sixty to seventy silver yuan.

Joining the Shanghai YWCA

In 1931, I joined the Shanghai Young Women Christian Association (YWCA), where I was assigned to the Labor Department as an industrial secretary. The Labor Department focused on female workers. At that time, Shanghai had numerous textile factories, resulting in a large population of female workers. Many of these workers were quite young, some as young as 13 or 14, and even 11-12-year-olds. Their work was physically demanding, and their lives were harsh. They often faced mistreatment and lived in challenging conditions.

The Labor (or Industrial) Department had both relief-oriented and legal assistance functions, but its most crucial role was establishing women's night schools. Funded by the YWCA, these schools hired teachers and were located in areas with concentrated female labor. The first school was situated on Xiaoshadu Road, with dormitories upstairs and classrooms downstairs. I, along with my colleague Deng Yuzhi and two foreign staff members, resided there. Across Shanghai, there were up to six women's night schools, with a total student population of 600-700. Since these schools were free and held classes in the evenings, word spread quickly when we posted announcements, attracting many students.

In the early 1930s, left-wing cultural and workers' movements influenced by the Chinese Communist Party were active in Shanghai. Consequently, many teachers and students at the women's night schools had communist affiliations or sympathies. While we sensed this, the YWCA generally refrained from intervening in their activities. The classes, songs taught, and theatrical performances leaned toward progressive ideals. As a result, numerous students from the YWCA women's night schools received significant intellectual and cultural enrichment. These young girls, who once couldn't even read, grew into active participants in the later anti-Japanese resistance movement. Many of them joined the New Fourth Army and became Communist Party cadres, while some bravely sacrificed their lives.

During this period, several events left a lasting impression:

1. Prominent Speakers and Educators:

    o In 1931, after the Mukden (奉天) Incident (September 18th Incident or 九一八事变) when Japan invaded Northeast China, the nationwide anti-Japanese movement gained momentum. Figures like Song Qingling, Yang Xingfo, and Lu Xun organized the Save the Nation Campaign. The Labor Department invited Ms. Shi Liang to

speak at the women's night school.
Additionally, educators such as Tao Xingzhi, Xia
Yan, Tian Han, Xian Xinghai, and Nie Er also
visited the school to teach songs and stage
plays. Xia Yan or Tian Han even collected
material for a literary work reflecting the
hardships of female workers, titled "Bao Shen
Gong (包身工)."

2. Frontline Support and Recognition:

    o   In 1932, during the Shanghai 19th Route Army's
        battle against Japanese invaders, the women's
        night school organized a frontline support
        delegation to visit and uplift the morale of
        fighting soldiers. They received an audience
        with General Chen Mingshu, the commander of
        the 19th Route Army.

3. Jiang Qing's Involvement:

    o   Jiang Qing (江青 then known as Teacher Li (李老
        師) was also a teacher at the women's night
        school. I remember she was introduced through
        Tao Xingzhi. She was young, tall, fair-skinned,
        and had a pleasant appearance. Although she

didn't teach classes, she actively participated in rehearsing plays and other activities. One day, a student informed me that Jiang Qing had been arrested. They asked me to notify her "in-laws." I visited an address provided by the student, which turned out to be a stone-gated house. A pale middle-aged woman in her forties or fifties answered the door. I informed her about Jiang Qing's arrest, and she didn't say much, simply went back inside. It seemed like a Communist Party liaison point. Within a week, Jiang Qing arrived at the YWCA Labor Department accompanied by two men in Western suits (typical attire for detectives in Shanghai). She still looked neat and attractive, and the two men seemed familiar with her. They asked if I knew Jiang Qing, and I mentioned that she was our women's night school teacher. They took her away again. I've never shared this story with anyone for decades. In 1956, after returning to China, I met with teachers and students from the women's night school and asked Zhang Shuyi about Jiang Qing's later situation. I also inquired if they wanted to invite Jiang Qing for a reunion. Zhang said that times had changed, and they no longer associated with her.

However, in October 1976, shortly after the downfall of the "Gang of Four," the Central Committee's special investigation team unexpectedly visited my home in Peking University's Yandong Garden (北大燕東園). They asked about Jiang Qing's arrest in Shanghai. After sharing what I knew, they asked how they found my location. Their response was surprising: "Jiang Qing's autobiography mentioned you during that period—Helen Chung (鍾韶琴)."

In 1935, the Shanghai YWCA established a policy that after five years of service, secretaries could receive funding for a one-year overseas visit and study. The procedure involved traveling first to the Soviet Union and then proceeding through Europe, ultimately arriving in New York by ship. At that time, the Soviet Union was the world's first socialist country, and my impressions were of cleanliness, orderliness, and ongoing construction. Children wore neatly pressed school uniforms, and various development projects were underway. However, during our stay in Moscow, some Soviet friends who visited us spoke cautiously, revealing an underlying tension. I later learned that this period coincided with internal struggles within the Soviet Communist Party against the Trotskyist faction. Our accommodations in hotels were uncomfortable due to the prevalence of large bedbugs.

Upon reaching the YWCA headquarters in New York, they arranged visits to successful YWCA activities in the eastern United States, with a particular focus on locations with labor departments. During this time, the United States was recovering from the Great Depression, and many workers faced unemployment and hardship. Basic necessities like eggs and sugar were rationed. Demonstrations, protests, and left-wing workers' movements were active. I enrolled in New York University for six months, studying economics. By the end of 1936, I returned to Shanghai. When I left, Zhang Shuyi (who later served as Vice Chair of the All-China Women's Federation and Chair of the China Women and Children Protection Association) had already arrived. In my absence, she managed my responsibilities, and when I returned, we worked together.

After the Lugou (蘆溝橋) Bridge Incident in July 1937, China entered a period of intense resistance against Japanese aggression. The Shanghai Anti-Japanese War began in August, 1937 disrupting the normal operations of women's night schools. Female students from these schools formed several service teams and went to the frontlines to rescue wounded soldiers, distribute relief supplies, and promote the resistance effort. Later, they collaborated with the progressive Lu Zhuoying unit. The New Fourth Army, led by Communist Party members Ye Ting and Xiang Ying, was established in southern Anhui, and many of these women joined its ranks. During the war, Shanghai faced Japanese bombings, resulting in a large refugee population, including many women and children suffering from hunger and homelessness. Consequently, the women's night schools transformed into refugee shelters, and the YWCA shifted its focus to assisting women and children.

I was appointed General Secretary of the YWCA in Kunming (昆明) at the end of 1937. Since Shanghai, except for the concessions, had fallen under Japanese occupation, our work there became impossible. A few of us decided to relocate to Kunming, Province of Yunnan (雲南). We traveled by ship from Shanghai to Hong Kong, then from Hong Kong to Haifeng, and finally took a train to Kunming. The journey was unsafe due to the ongoing conflict, and the train only operated during daylight hours, stopping at stations overnight. It took four days and nights to reach Kunming. During the train ride, I met Xie Bingxin (謝冰心), whom I already knew, and also became acquainted with Chen Yi (陳意). In Kunming, Chen Yi initially served as the dormitory supervisor for Southwest Associated University's (西

65

南聯大) female students. Later, for reasons unknown to me, she returned to Shanghai. As the YWCA General Secretary in Kunming, I received some funding from the YWCA headquarters in the United States. Jin Longzhang (金龙章), a Chinese capitalist, and his wife had relocated their textile factory to Kunming. His wife had previously served as a YWCA board member in Shanghai and frequently made donations. She arrived in Kunming before me and later invited me to oversee the YWCA there. Through their connections, I also established relationships with prominent figures in Kunming, including Long Yun (龙云, the Governor of Yunnan) and Miao Yuntai's (缪云台) wife. We held annual board meetings, seeking their assistance in sponsoring our work. Initially, the Labor Department also opened a women's night school near Jin Longzhang's factory. However, due to the scarcity of workers in Kunming, their dispersed living arrangements, and the lack of suitable teachers, the school closed shortly after opening.

In this way, the YWCA's focus shifted to young students. At that time, the Southwest Associated University (西南聯大, SWAU), formed by Tsinghua University, Peking University, and Nankai University, was located in Kunming. Additionally, many universities and secondary schools had relocated from coastal areas to escape the Japanese invasion. The student population was substantial, but most had lost contact with their families due to war disruptions. Their lives were challenging—many suffered from malnutrition, inadequate food, and poor health, with tuberculosis affecting a significant number.

The Kunming YWCA, where I was serving as the General Secretary, established affordable female student dormitories to accommodate these young women. They also organized soy milk production, providing free soy milk to students at SWAU, Yunnan University, and other institutions. Many people fondly remembered this soy milk, including He Dongchang, who later served as the president of Tsinghua University and the Minister of Education. The Kunming YWCA's soy milk gained popularity, and Li Feng and her team further developed it into "soybean powder," a convenient drink that could be prepared by simply adding water. This nutritious supplement was distributed to students suffering from tuberculosis and even to children in society who lacked access to milk. The Kunming YWCA played a significant role in these efforts.

Additionally, during winter, the Kunming YWCA distributed warm cotton coats to young students. Kunming's high-altitude location made winters quite cold, and these coats were essential. Every year, the Kunming YWCA used donations to produce a batch of coats for students in need. Some students also received financial assistance. While not a complete solution, it eased their immediate hardships.

Beyond student-focused work, the Kunming YWCA also had divisions for girls and women. The Girls' Division assisted unmarried women facing difficulties, while the Family Women's Division helped women experiencing family-related challenges. The Kunming YWCA mobilized social resources to provide aid to those in need.

After World War II, many people in Kunming emigrated to the United States until China's liberation in 1949. When I left Kunming in 1945, the Chinese resistance against Japan had not yet achieved victory yet but was in sight. I traveled first to India by plane, where I witnessed the extreme poverty of laborers under British rule. From there, I boarded a ship in Calcutta, heading to the United States. While waiting for the ship, news arrived of Japan's surrender. Once the ship arrived, the journey felt much safer. Upon reaching New York, I discovered that Jin Longzhang, his wife, and Wang Qixin (the General Secretary of the Men's YWCA) had also arrived in the United States.

I pursued a master's degree in education at Columbia University. After graduating, I married Mr. Yen-lin Teng (鄧衍林) and focused on family life. I passed the United Nations' examination and became a staff member, serving as a liaison officer for non-governmental organizations in the Far East region. Gradually, I distanced myself from the YWCA. In 1956, I returned to China with my husband and children and began a new chapter of life, working at Peking University and the National Library in Beijing.

(The descriptions above are based on a recording of Ms. Helen Chung's speech, recorded by and assisted in editing by Mr. Xu Weizhong (許維中 husband of Rosaline S. Teng Xu), in June 2003, just before Helen Chung's 100th birthday.)

Our Family Stories by Henry S. Teng

Introduction

Our father, Yen-lin Teng (鄧衍林), and mother, Helen Chung Teng

(鍾韶琴), responded to the call of Premier Zhou Enlai (周恩來) in

October 1956 and brought the whole family back to China. After

our father returned to China, he became an associate professor

in the Department of Library Science of Peking University (北京

大學圖書館學系). We lived in a courtyard house at No. 8 Tongfuyi

(佟府乙八號) on the campus of Peking University (北京大學，it is

said this place was the former Yenching University Women's

Clinic). The Peking University red guards during the Cultural

Revolution forcibly moved us to No. 22, Yandong Garden (燕東

園), Peking University, in 1967.

Figure 15 Photo of the family taken in New York City in about 1950: Prof. Yen-lin Teng, Helen Chung Teng, Henry Shao-lin Teng, and Rosaline Shao-yun Teng.

Our father grew up in a poor family in his early years, and he worked in the Jiangxi (江西) Provincial Library from 1927 to 1930. He graduated from Wuchang Wenhua (武昌文華) Library Management Vocational College in the early 1930s and entered Peking's National Library (北京圖書館) for employment. He graduated from Southwest Associated University (西南聯大) in early 1941. In the periodization of scholars in library science in China, he is usually regarded as the "second generation of scholars", that is, "the generation of Wenhua". During the Anti-Japanese War, our father co-founded Kunming Tianxiang Middle School (天祥中學) with several Jiangxi classmates in Kunming and became the first and founding principal/head of the school. After the victory of the Anti-Japanese War, he went to the United States to study and obtained a master's degree from the Teachers College of Columbia University in 1946. He then worked at the Secretariat of the United Nations (Headquarters) in New York, USA. My sister Rosaline Teng (or Deng Shao-yun 鄧少莣) and myself were born in Manhattan, New York during this period.

The academic research of father's past works has been relatively active in the development history of Library Science. Among them, Professor Zhou Yujiao (周余嬌) from the Institute of Ancient Books Conservation of Tianjin Normal University has conducted many in-depth and detailed investigations and researches, and published several academic papers. Among them, in her research report "Deng Yan-lin's (or Yen-lin Teng's) Life, Writings and Contributions"[32], she described father's academic contributions as follows:

> Deng Yanlin (Yen-lin Teng) has traveled to many universities and institutions at home and abroad throughout his life and has mainly engaged in library science and education. His personal experience is not insignificant. It is generally believed that "Deng has been engaged in library science teaching and practical work all

his life, and has rich theoretical and practical experiences, especially in bibliography." His views on the relationship between library science and bibliography also have certain reference value. He has a wide range of interests. In the process of compiling the catalog, he has been involved in natural science and social science, including ancient books of literature and history, economy, education, frontier (China national boarders) geography, chemistry, mathematics, engineering, etc. He indeed lives up to the honor of a "general reference librarian". Reputation-wise, he is also recognized as a "reference expert". This article makes a preliminary exploration of Deng Yanlin's (Yen-lin Teng's) life, writings and contributions. Regarding Deng Yanlin's (Yen-lin Teng's) achievements in catalog compilation, catalog nationalization, and reference consultation, it is worth further in-depth research. For example, he served in the United Nations and taught in the Department of Library Science of Peking University. Yet there are still some gaps in this aspect, and we look forward to further research these areas in the future.

Encouraging Us to Develop in Multiple Areas

From an early age our father encouraged us as kids to develop ourselves in a variety of areas. I remember when we were eight or nine years old, our father drove us nearly an hour to a dancing school in New York City to learn modern dance. After learning some basic dancing moves, the teacher asked us to dance to the music for five to ten minutes based on our imagination to a depicted topic. I remember that one of my subjects at that time was "a construction worker building buildings". So, I imitated some scenes I saw on TV, while dancing, swinging an imaginary hammer and laying imaginary bricks, and danced for a few minutes. The dance teacher was so impressed by my dancing act that she arranged for a few senior students to sit in and observe my performance. Naturally, I was quite proud of myself. I recall that every time after the dancing class, my father would take us to enjoy ice cream as encouragement. Later on, as I grew up, I gradually lost interest in dancing. Maybe as part of a little boy's psychological growth, and I didn't want to perform in public any more. It even reached the point of "rebellion against any performance of dancing".

Figure 16 Father working at the United Nations Headquarters (秘書處) in New York City during the 1950s.

When we were a little bit older, my father often took us to participate in various outdoor activities, such as fishing, crabbing, swimming and so on. I remember once the whole family went fishing for crabs in a river in the suburbs of New York, and caught nearly a hundred crabs, large and small, in one day. After returning home, our parents and friends enjoyed a big meal of crabs. We had to give the remaining crabs to our neighbors. My father's influence fostered my love for nature and outdoor activities.

Figure 17 Father taught us how to fish.

In 1956, our parents brought the whole family back to China. Father was teaching as a professor in the Department of Library Science of Peking University. After father returned to China, he was busy at teaching at Peking University and various activities in the library science field. I became interested in assembling radios out of mine stones (礦石收音機), electronic vacuum tubes, and bipolar junction transistors (BJT) in fifth grade. My father was very supportive of my exploration. He strongly encouraged me to go to the Haidian Xinhua Bookstore to buy relevant books to study and increase my knowledge in electronics, and go to hardware stores to buy various electronic components. These included electronic vacuum tubes, semiconductor diodes, semiconductor triodes, resistors, and capacitors. Of course, what my father didn't know was that I had to climb up to the roof of our one story-high house in order to install an antenna to get stronger radio broadcasting signals. Perhaps I was too daring at that age to climb up and ignore the consequences of rolling down the roof. Fortunately, the fall never happened!

Our Encounter with Premier Zhou Enlai (周恩來)

When my father was teaching at Peking University, due to the timing of his return to China in 1956 and the field of scientific information management, he met with Premier Zhou Enlai (周恩來) three times and talked about the current situation and future development of the library/information industry in China and abroad.

At the end of July and the beginning of August 1958, the government arranged for our family to go to Beidaihe (北戴河) for vacation. On August 9th, when we were having lunch at the hotel where we were staying, it happened that Premier Zhou Enlai and his wife Deng Yingchao (鄧穎超) and his party came to the hotel where we were staying for dinner. Because father had talked about work with Premier Zhou before, my father walked forward to say hello to Premier Zhou and started a dialogue about the current situation of the library/information industry. My brother, Deng Yunsheng (鄧云生), my sister, Rosaline Teng (鄧少钰), and myself, the three of us, rushed upstairs to get our diary notebook. We came down to ask for Premier Zhou's signature as a souvenir. Premier Zhou, while putting his signature down on the notebooks, asked us about our life and schooling in English. Although we were born and had lived in the United States for eight or nine years, and we had only been back to China for less than two years, we couldn't speak a word of English! We were very ashamed of ourselves. My father quickly explained that we no longer spoke English at home anymore, because English was the language spoken by the American imperialists! Premier Zhou laughed out loud, and then kindly mentioned to us to study English well, because it is a useful tool for rebuilding China.

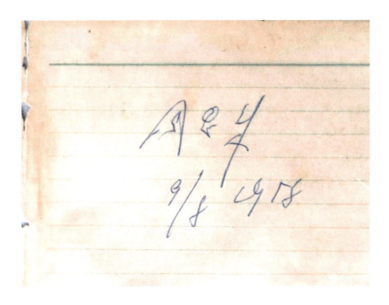

Figure 18 Premier Zhou En-lai left his signature in a notebook of brother Deng Yun-sheng (鄧云生).

From then on, the three of us, under private teaching of our parents particularly my mother, persisted in studying English at home every Sunday for four years until high schools started to offer English classes. These four years of supplementary lessons in English have benefited us a lot and laid the foundation for our future development not only in English as a language, but career development as well, unknown to us then.

Figure 19 Family photo taken in the mid-1960s.

Our Parents' Ups and Downs in the Cultural Revolution

My father came from the pre-revolutionary society (prior to 1949, when China was ruled by the Nationalists), later went to the United States to study, and lived in the United States for ten years before returning to China in 1956. At the beginning of the Cultural Revolution in 1966, the people and society in China were led by slogans such as "Sweep Away All Monsters and Demons (横扫一切牛鬼蛇神)", "Destroy the old to establish the new (破旧立新)". This is a period of intense political and social upheaval in China during the mid-20th century. My father and our home at Tongfu, Peking University soon became the targets of the Red Guards' revolution.

When we returned to China, the HR policies of the United Nations Headquarters at that time said that, for returning/retiring personnel to their home country, all relocation expenses, including travel expenses, moving of furniture, appliances, bikes, personal stuff, even our American toys, were paid by the United Nations. Letters from our relatives in China said that New China (after take-over by the Chinese Communist Party) had just started and the material conditions were poor. So, it would be wise to bring more western things back home to China. I recall that my parents went on a shopping expedition and bought a full set of trendy living room sofas, kitchen dining sets, bedroom furniture sets, foam-based beds, a tape recorder, a refrigerator, advanced radios, and other electrical appliances and heavy-duty transformers (1000 watts for the refrigerator for one). At that time, my parents had decided not to bring a TV set back to China, mainly because China's TV broadcasting system (NTSC vs. PAL) was still undecided. Plus, they noticed that we spent too much time watching TV programs and not studying hard enough.

Later during the Cultural Revolution, the consequence of this whole-house move-back to China, including our children's various dolls, American western cowboy fake pistols and other toys became the "ironclad evidence" of our father's guilt of " Worshipping Everything Foreign".

Figure 20 Father and son/author taken in 1973.

The Red Guards took turns to destroy anything old and anything foreign. First, the ones from Peking University took important documents of ours from the United States, including the birth certificates of my sister and me in the United States, and a bulky 18" x 12" audio tape recorder back to the Library Science Department of Peking University.

As the mass movement of the revolution moved forward, Red Guards from all over China began to connect and learn from each other. Their first stop was Peking University as a must to learn the essence from the best exemplars of Red Guards at Peking University, the most significant center of the Red Guard movement lit up by Chaiman Mao and his wife Jiang Qing. My home was located behind the Courtyard #3, #4, #5, and #6, where the Party and university administration departments of Peking University had their offices. These locations became the natural places to post all kinds of so-called big-character posters (大字報) that supposedly uncovered and exposed the crimes and evils of feudalism, capitalism, and revisionism of the university administrators. There were even more posters posted at the Big Dining Hall (大飯廳) for the Peking University students. There was an endless stream of people who came to our house. There were also those who posted big-character posters and those who read big-character posters. At that time, I was living in the dorms of my high school. When I returned home every week or two, a group of Red Guards, who came from nowhere, were criticizing my parents in a public setting. There were dozens of them. I witnessed my parents wearing demeaning top hats, having their arms pulled back, and standing in a "jet" like posture. Someone even poured flour-based glue over their heads to humiliate them. When I saw this scene, I was very frightened and powerless. I decided not to stay long, and went back to school through a back door.

During the Cultural Revolution, people took pride in "exposing" others. A neighbor of ours lived in a unit separated from my father's office room by a wall. She was not very literate, so she probably asked someone to write a big-character poster, exposing my father as an American spy. She claimed that she often heard someone was sending telegrams in the middle of a night on the other side of the wall, as she heard the typical di-di-da sound of hitting the telegram key with her own ears. Unfortunately, we indeed brought back from the United States a Zenith black radio with all bands including shortwave bands, and an extendable one-meter-high antenna. When the Red Guards in the Library Science Department of Peking University read the big-character posters on the exposures, they reacted quickly. They ransacked the house, discovered the Zenith black radio and immediately suspected that the Zenith radio might had had the function of sending and receiving telegrams. Afterwards, there were endless confrontations about the reported event, questioning my father in harsh tones many times about possible espionage activities with American intelligent agencies.

My father repeatedly explained that he had the habit of working in the middle of the night. He often uses a portable typewriter to type some index cards in Western languages. This is the normal work of cataloging books in Western languages, and has nothing to do with transmitting messages via a shortwave radio. After the Red Guards carefully checked out the radio and typewriter, they found that these devices were indeed ordinary, and decided to let it go. The radio, typewriter and some personal documents were all returned to my father a year later. Only the audio tape recorder was taken away and never returned, because it was very useful for its "high technology" at the time. As for the Zenith multi-band radio, my sister and me took it to the countryside of Wutong Village in Shan Xi Providence (山西省梧桐村) during our stay as young students doing farm work (插隊知識青年). Of course, the radio added some fun to our classmates' daily life, thirty-one of us to be precise, in our living quarters among miles of farmland and crops.

My father was originally in good health, full of energy, and able to stay up late. But years of hard work and intense work caused him to suffer from severe gastric ulcer and vertigo in the United States. In 1962, when I was in junior high school, my father was diagnosed with suspected gastric cancer again and had to remove the cancer through surgery. Unfortunately, my father was told right before the surgery that the senior surgeon was switched to his assistant on the spur of the moment to operate on father. What followed was a medical accident, and father had to undergo another two surgeries to address the damage caused by the accident. In the end, his body couldn't bear the multiple operations anymore. He was seeing the doctors often, was taking all kinds of medicine, and earned the nick name in our family as the "medicine jar (藥罐子)".

During the storm of the Cultural Revolution in January 1967, the Red Guards, or rebels (造反派) as they call themselves, seized administration and management power of the school. They began to drive the school mass movement in depth, promoting the ideology of "Suspect everything, and touch the soul". The rebel faction in power in the department began to increase the intensity of attacks against father, asking him repeatedly why he wanted to return to China. They questioned whether "he was truly patriotic or simply traitorous", and asked father to dig deeper into his soul for answers. My father "confessed" in a matter-of-fact manner that both of my father and mother had participated in a study group organized by a local progressive Chinese organization in the United States. They also had received letters from relatives in China about the new social changes in China and the need for expertise in science and technology.

From 1955 to 1956, father read articles in the newspapers run by local Chinese that Premier Zhou Enlai was calling on Chinese scientists, experts, specialists, and scholars abroad to return to China to build a new China. He heard rumors that Professor Qian Xuesen (錢學森) returned to China in twists and turns. My parents were interviewed and vetted several times by the FBI of the US government. Father described his motivation for returning to China in this way: "In October 1956, I resigned from my permanent employment secured by a lifetime contract at the United Nations Secretariat. I returned to China with my whole family in response to the Party's (Chinese Communist Party or CPP) call to participate in the socialist revolution and China reconstruction, and serve the people."

However, no matter how my father explained the reasons for returning to China, the rebels, or the "young revolutionaries" in my father's own words, did not believe it. They firmly believed that it was impossible to sacrifice all the goodies of life for patriotism, when a person has a good income in the United States, an iron rice bowl (meaning secure job or 鐵飯碗), a car, a single-family house with a garden and a swimming pool, etc. There had to be some ulterior reason, so the Red Guards came to the conclusion that father pretended to show patriotism to hide his traitorous acts.

My mother really couldn't stand this kind of torture. Considering that she had a special working relationship with Jiang Qing (江青) at the Shanghai Young Women's Association (YWCA) in the 1930s, she wanted to write a letter of clarification to Jiang Qing. Jiang was then the Deputy Director in the Central Cultural Revolution Group (中央文革小組付組長), an extremely powerful group of people during the revolution, and asked for help. The time was around February 1967. I was recuperating at home with acute hepatitis. I often heard my parents and my fourth uncle, Professor Zhong Yuanzhao (鍾元昭), discussing the matter. My fourth uncle helped to write the letter draft, because he was working as an editor/translator for English and Russian translation to Chinese at the Science & Technology Publishing House (科學技術出版社). He was quick in writing and coming up with drafts of the letter for further discussions.

My mother, Helen Chung Teng (鍾韶琴), graduated from the Sociology Department of Shanghai Hujiang University (上海滬江大學) in 1931. From 1931 to August 1938, she worked as an industrial secretary (勞工幹事) in the Labor Department (勞工部) of the Shanghai YWCA. In 1935, she went to Moscow, the Soviet Union at that time, for a short investigation of their society. After a short stay, she traveled to New York City, USA to attend a conference of the World YWCA. In the 1940s, under the influence of Li Gongpu (李公樸) and Li Wenxuan (李文宣), she joined the China Democratic League (中国民主同盟). Many years later in the 1980s, she served as a member of the Central Liaison Committee of the China Democratic League, an advisor to the All-China Women's Federation, and a member of the Sixth National Committee of the Chinese People's Political Consultative Conference (中國全国政治协商委员会).

At the end of 1929, with the support of the China National Association of YWCA, the Shanghai YWCA established a labor service office completely run by the YWCA itself in places where female workers were concentrated. The purpose was to learn more about the situation of female workers, to solve their problems through education, and to train more social service personnel to meet the needs of female workers. Mother happened to graduate from college at this time. During her school days, she paid attention to issues such as labor, capital and women, and was soon employed by the Shanghai Young Women's Association as an industrial secretary in their Labor Department. The article "Christian Church and Labor Issues (基督教會與劳工问题)"[33] describes the situation of the YWCA night school for female workers and mother's involvement as the following:

"In 1930, the Shanghai YWCA rented two apartments in Sanheli, Xiaoshadu Road (小沙渡路三和里) (today known as

#21- 23, 910 Long, Xikang Street or 西康路 910 弄 21-23 号),
to hold the Huxi Women Workers' Club (滬西女工社). The
downstairs was for the classroom and extracurricular
activities for the women's night school, and the upstairs
served as a dormitory for the cadres and teachers of the
Labor Department. Helen Chung (鍾韶琴), an industrial
secretary of the Labor Department of the Shanghai YWCA,
and Bai Meili (May Bagwell or 白美丽) moved into
residence at the outset".

It was at this time that mother met Jiang Qing and called her
Teacher Li. Around 1999, I asked my mother about Jiang Qing's
arrest in Shanghai in the 1930s. She recalled that Teacher Li at
that time had fair skin and worked in the night school for female
workers. One day my mother was asked to visit a person in a
prison in Shanghai. Mother did not remember exactly who
called or whether the name of her colleague was mentioned.
But mother said that it was Teacher Li/Jiang Qing whom she
met in the Shanghai prison. I remember mom's story very
clearly. Moreover, Jiang Qing specially asked mother to drop a
note to Li's "mother-in-law(婆婆)" at home. Mother could only
assume that this message she relayed about Jiang's arrest
eventually made its way to the local CCP.

According to the book "The Rise and Fall of the Gang of Four" (by Ye Yonglie) (《四人帮兴亡》作著叶永烈), Jiang Qing was "arranged to work at Shanghai Pudong as a teacher by the YWCA. Jiang Qing was assigned to a dormitory in the factory area, and she herself had a room in the back. The front portion of the house was used as a classroom, and the female workers lived in another house nearby." Presumably, mother knew Jiang Qing's living address from the YWCA's records of employees, and successfully passed the message about Jiang's arrest to Jiang Qing's "mother-in-law".

In 1956, our family returned to China and took a train to Fuzhou (福州), my mother's hometown, to visit her parents (Zhong Chunhui (锺春晖), Xue Peiying (薛佩英), my grandpa and grandma), whom she hadn't seen for more than ten years. We passed through Shanghai, where we met several female workers, a few teachers of the previous Shanghai YWCA night school for female workers, and Ms. Deng Yuzhi (Cora Deng or 邓裕志). Ms. Cora Deng was my mother's previous leader and the executive industrial secretary of the Shanghai Young Women's Association. When my mother asked about Teacher Li during conversations with former students and teachers, she learned that Teacher Li had changed her name to Jiang Qing. These veteran cadres (老干部) advised my mother not to see Teacher Li, as it was inconvenient for her since Teacher Li married Chairman Mao Zedong (毛澤東) and became Mrs. Mao. Mother listened to their advice without a question.

Because my mother had this relationship with Jiang Qing, she thought of writing a letter to Jiang and asking for help in an unsettling situation. After a while, I never heard my parents discuss the matter of writing letters anymore. Fortunately, this letter was never sent, otherwise I don't know what more suffering and hardship would have come.

Pushing Us to Strive for a College Education

As part of their wishes in returning to China, my parents wanted us to get a college degree. Their guiding principle, particularly my father's, was to get a better education that would lead to a better job.

My elder brother Deng Yunsheng (鄧云生) from my father's first marriage, got into college before the Cultural Revolution and graduated from the Department of Water Conservancy and Electric Power of Tsinghua University (清華大學). In 1968, he was assigned to work in Guangdong (廣東).

My sister Rosaline Teng and I got caught up with the Cultural Revolution chaos in high school and went to Xiaoyi County (孝義縣), Shanxi Province (山西省) to work in the countryside as young farmers at the end of 1968 and the beginning of 1969. My sister did well in the countryside, got into the Physics Department of Shanxi University (山西大學), graduated with a B.S. degree in Radio Technology (a hot major then), and was assigned to work in a Beijing TV Factory.

After my stay in the countryside for a couple of years, I was transferred back officially to the municipal city of Beijing (北京市) in April 1972. Bear in mind that China has a very strict residential registration system (戶口制度) to limit the residential population of cities. After returning to Beijing, my path to full employment was full of twists and turns including my contract or temporary job of teaching English at Bayi Middle School (八一中學) in Haidian District (海淀區), Beijing. After working as a temporary worker in a plastic molding factory for a couple of months, I was officially assigned to work in the Information & Technology Office of the Institute of Chemistry (化學所科學技術情報室), Academy of Sciences of China (中國科學院) as an English translator.

In 1978, China resumed its national university unified examination and enrollment. I hesitated or down right rejected the idea to take the national college unified entrance examination and apply for colleges. After years in the countryside, I just got married with Liu Chang-hou (劉昌厚 or Joan Teng) in Beijing in 1977, found a good job at the Institute of Chemistry, and very much had settled down. And I was thirty-one years old, not an optimal age for college studies, I thought to myself. Father and mother were travelling to and visiting their home towns in Nanchang, Jiangxi (南昌，江西省) and Fuzhou and Quanzhou, Fujian (福州和泉州，福建省). My father spent an awful amount of time urging us (me and Joan) in long letters to take the entrance examinations. He also copied more than ten pages of math questions and problems as exercises and sent them to our home in Beijing. Under my father's unremitting encouragement, I changed my mind, took the entrance examination, applied, and was admitted to the English Teacher Class (Teaching English as a Secondary Language) of the Graduate School of the Chinese Academy of Sciences in 1978 (中科院研究生院/英語師資班 1978), under the guidance of Professor Li Pei (李佩教授) of the University of Science and Technology of China (中國科技大學). My wife Liu Changhou was also admitted to Beijing Institute of Civil Engineering and Architecture (北京建築工程學院). From then on, I began my life as a college student at the age of thirty-one.

Figure 21 Father and son/author taken at the Summer Palace (頤和園) in Beijing in 1975.

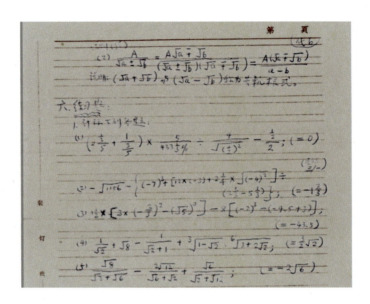

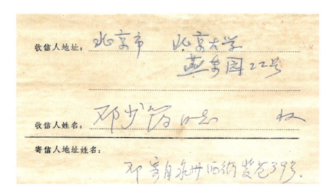

Figure 22 Father copied math exercises by hand to encourage us to take the national college entrance examinations.

96

In the summer of 1979, I had been studying at the Graduate School of the Chinese Academy of Sciences for a year, and a couple of my classmates applied for and successfully were admitted into graduate schools abroad such as Singapore.

During a conversation with my father, he learned that I was also considering this study path abroad. Father had been tracking the application of computers in his field of scientific information & management in the past few years. He saw computer science as a promising field for studies. He encouraged me to try to apply for graduate schools at several American universities. I wrote a few letters of inquiries with his recommendation letters. However, the graduate school application letters led nowhere, because I did not study science nor had a diploma from a Chinese university to show my education credentials.

When I was doing translation work in the Institute of Chemistry, I supported the researchers as an English translator. When the researchers imported and had an advanced mass spectrometer from the UK to be installed in their lab, I had my first encounter with a medium-sized or minicomputer from the United States for data collection and analysis. I gained an understanding of and interest in what computers could do.

While studying to become an English teacher for the Graduate School of the Chinese Academy of Sciences, I recalled how the researchers would use a computer to do their scientific data acquisitions and analysis equipped with their education background. I came to the conclusion that I had no choice but to start my studies at the undergraduate course level. This was not an easy change of thought on schooling, because I was thirty-two years old then. I kept asking myself whether I could make the transition from college studies as a freshman.

Figure 23 Father and son/author working on a college application to a university in the United States in 1979.

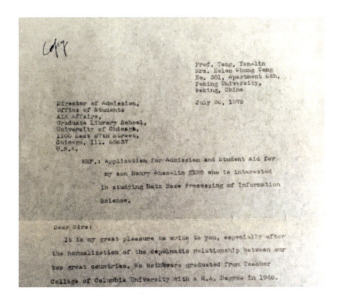

Figure 24 Father wrote a recommendation letter to the Admission Office of the University of Chicago.

In the early autumn of 1979, my father was hospitalized for esophageal cancer at the Beijing Hospital (北京醫院). Our cousin Ms. Jin Liang-juan (荆良娟) made the arrangement for father to get admitted into this hospital mainly for high-ranking officers.

In September, 1979, Major Henry Biehusen and Mrs. Sally Biehusen, old friends of my parents, who lived in Palm Beach, Florida in the United States, came to Beijing to visit our family as tourists. Mrs. Biehusen, who had nursed me in my infancy and was my god-mother in childhood, had a very deep affection for me.

Figure 25 Major & Mrs. Henry & Sally Biehusen, father, mother, and Henry Jr.,
the author, in New York City in 1947.

Prior to their visit to Beijing, former U.S. president Nixon made
a visit to China in 1972 and opened the door for renewed
friendly visits between the two countries. In order to find my
parents, which they hadn't communicated with for over sixteen
years since 1956, the Biehusen couple wrote a letter to the
Chinese Embassy in Canada. In their letter they inquired about
the whereabouts of the Teng family in China. They actually
made an effort to go through their congressman in Florida to
initiate the inquiry. Their inquiry received a response from the
Chinese Embassy in Canada. The response explained that
father's name in English as Yen-lin Teng was insufficient to
identify the person in China, because the spelling might
correspond to a number of different characters in Chinese. They

needed father's name in Chinese. Fortunately, the Biehusens found a celebration card of my naming after Major Henry Biehusen that bore father's name in Chinese as "鄧衍林". They responded with a copy of the celebration card.

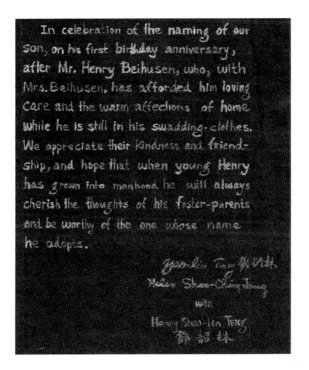

Figure 26 Celebration card in 1948 that bears father's name in Chinese as "鄧衍林".

The celebration card response worked and they received the address of the Department of Library Science of Peking University (北京大學圖書館學系) offered by the Foreign Experts Bureau of the Chinese State Council (中國國務院外國专家局). The Biehusen couple wrote their first letter to contact our parents.

The timing was in the late period of the Cultural Revolution around 1974. Shao-lin (or Henry) remembers that our parents were both happy and scared when they were handed over this first letter from the Department head. Our parents were happy that the Biehusen couple did not forget the friendship with their old friends in China, but our parents were afraid that they would be suspected again of being in contact with a foreign intelligence agency or spy. After discussing the matter with the Department leadership of Peking University, mother carefully replied and wrote a letter in English. Many years later, Shao-lin talked with the Biehusen couple about this event. They said that they were overjoyed when they received a letter from our parents in Beijing. They knew that mother's English was always very good. After all, she was well educated in English at a missionary high school. Further she studied at the Department of Sociology of Shanghai Hujiang University (上海滬江大學 now Shanghai University of Science and Technology). They sensed the unspeakable between the lines in the letter.

On September 28, 1979, Major Henry Biehusen and Mrs. Sally Biehusen (or Uncle Henry and Aunt Sally as we called them) came to Beijing Hospital to see our father. They took pictures in front of the hospital bed. The old friends hadn't seen each other for 23 years since 1956, so everyone was naturally very excited. In the ensuing hour-long conversation, father explained Shao-lin's (or Henry's) interest in studying computer science and gave his support of the idea and drive. Father hoped that the Biehusen couple could help to make it happen. Father also wrote a letter in English to express his sustenance or wishes. At that time, father had undergone cancer radiation therapy and chemotherapy, and was very weak. He revised the hand-written letter back and forth, and wasn't very keen on the exact date due to the side effects of the various cancer treatments. The Biehusen couple agreed to my father's death-bed wishes from their hearts and became my financial guarantor and supporter for my studies in the United States.

Figure 27 Father, who was terminally ill, mother, and Major & Mrs. Biehusen at the Beijing Hospital (北京醫院).

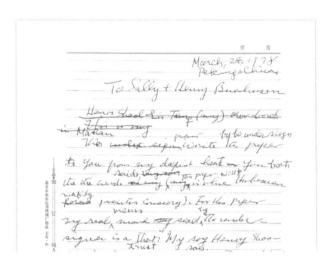

Figure 28 The letter father wrote to Major & Mrs. Biehusen in his hospital bed.

Around April 1980, I received undergraduate admission letters from seven or eight universities and applied for a Chinese passport to study in the United States. I remember every time I went to visit father, he would ask about the progress of the U.S. college application and passport application. Father asked about the matter so many times that I had to simply show him the college acceptance letter and passport. Father was satisfied and never asked again. Father took to his heart about my studies in Computer Science until he passed away at the end of April, 1980.

In September 1980, I went to Northeastern University in Boston, USA to study Computer Science as a college freshman. Uncle

Henry and Aunt Sally saw me off at an airport in Philadelphia, after attending a friend's daughter's wedding event. Then David Chen, Chang-hou's cousin, came to pick me up at Logan Airport, Boston, and arranged to have me stay with his wife, Crystal, and their very young kids, Paul and Brian. I lived with the Chen family for a week or so before heading to classes at Northeastern University. I am extremely grateful to both the Biehusens and Chens for their help and generosity in getting me restarted in the U.S.A.

In the following years from 1980 to 1986, I studied, worked, and obtained a B.S. degree from Northeastern University and an M.S. degree from Worcester Polytechnic Institute (also known as WPI in Massachusetts) in Computer Science. After graduation, I worked for several well-known American technology companies, such as Digital Equipment Corporation or DEC, Charles Schwab, eBay, and Philips (https://www.usa.philips.com/), obtained three patents[34] that were approved and granted by the US Patent Office, made contributions to Cybersecurity protection and the application of artificial intelligence to information security[35], and fulfilled father's last wishes.

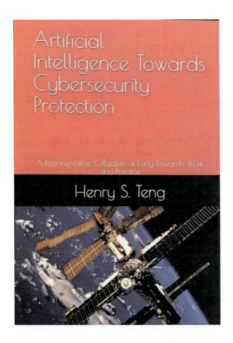

Figure 29 A book published by Henry Teng of more than three hundred pages on applying Artificial Intelligence to Cybersecurity.

Postface

Our mother, Helen Chung Teng (鍾韶琴), conducted home visits to women workers in the 1930s in Shanghai, delving into their working and living conditions. She successfully integrated the process of teaching literacy with the practical work and lives of these women.

Figure 30 Mother Helen Chung Teng taken in New York City in 1946.

Figure 31 Mother Helen Chung Teng in the 1980s.

Mother dedicated her youth as an educator and leader to women workers in Shanghai during the 1930s. Her efforts went beyond mere teaching; she connected literacy education with the practical realities of these women's lives.

Even half a century later, her students in the 1930s continue to express their deepest gratitude for her tireless dedication. Through multiple social gatherings and heartfelt letters exchanged with her past students/workers and fellow teachers of that era, their appreciation remains strong and sincere.

In one of those letters dated January 14, 1993, they wrote to mother and affectionately referred to her as their "gardener (園丁)". The students/workers fondly remembered and appreciated mother's nurturing care and hard work in cultivating their minds.

Among the pinkish pages, heartfelt letters addressed to
"Teacher Chung (鍾先生)" expressed deep longing and profound
appreciation. The students thanked their beloved "gardener"
for nurturing their minds, even decades later. Their wishes for
peace, happiness, and longevity resonated across the years.

The closing lines in their letter convey warm wishes for peace,
happiness, and longevity:
    "May each year be safe and joyful!"
    "May blessings be as vast as the Eastern Sea!"
    "May life be as enduring as the Southern Mountains!"

The precious photographs below have captured a moment of
gratitude and connection between teacher and students.
Mother's impact on her students' lives echoes through time,
and their heartfelt sentiments continue to resonate.

邓先出——我们亲爱的园丁们

　　我们在深深地想念妳 无
限感激妳. 铭记妳辛劳培育我
们的恩情! 遥祝

　　岁岁平安! 年年快乐

　　福如东海; 寿比南山!

　　　　　妳的女工夜校
　　　　　全体学生敬上 83.1.14

　　邓先出在此致 亲切的问候。
她身体健康. 生活很快乐. 阴阿姨
照应. 还有30年代同学—施桢 仍然然
陪伴. 为她读报信……
　　　　　　　　　　又及

110

向老师报告近况

女工夜校在上海的老师去有200多人。最高龄邓先生93岁,最轻的年纪也65岁了。平常每週1下午1－4时有少数人来联系联系,如得知谁身体欠佳,我赶去慰问。有听报告(名人、专家)就有较多人来参加。每年春节大联欢总有百余人参加。情况热烈,气氛亲切;既歌又舞,赞颂深厚的友谊及园丁灌溉丰获的成果。

亲爱的亲戚、朋友们：林琼，里路，丁宁，李淑英，胡瑞蕊

新年好！1997是我们这10年生活变化较大的一年。

少林97年年中财从美国东岸波士顿 Fidelity 投资公司换工作到了西岸加州旧金山 Charles Schwab 投资公司作 Managing Director。主管整个公司的计算机网络保密通讯及安全的工程开发。事业上责任多了，待遇也有了增加。利用公司的福利，我们因而从波士顿搬到了旧金山海湾区。Charles Schwab 公司成立于1974年。其宗旨在于提供证券投资者低价而全面的投资选择。Schwab 在全美各地共设有240多家分行，客户资产超过三千五百亿美元，并提供24小时华语服务。

昌厚仍在 IBM/Lotus 工作。她的部门让她通过网络在加州工作。每一到两个月回波士顿一趟。对于这样一个安排，她倒感到自由愉快。

从波士顿搬到加州，是我们考虑多年的战略转移。人到了一定年令更珍惜生活中的各个方面，更把人生想干的事情付之行动。我们这次搬迁，也就是遂了自己多年的心愿。我们在半年内完成了调换工作，卖房买房，跨岸搬家的大变动。到目前为止，确实感到加州从天气，工作机会，中美文化，是难以再有的结合。除房价外，其他都很令人满意。等我们安顿好了以后，会更充份的享受这边的一切。

少林妈妈这两年一直和我们住在一起。这次到了加州，她见到了几位40年没见面的老朋友，真是高兴极了。她今年93岁高龄，行动自理，脑子清楚。中文报纸，美国影到片，中国系到片，成了她每天的生活内容。加州天气温和，对老年人非常适益。

我们很想知道我们的亲戚朋友们这一年过的怎麼样。虽然通信不多，你们却是我们生活中常常想到的一部分。加州离大陆更近了，希望你们有机会时来相聚畅谈。

祝大家在新的一年里，身体健康，事业有成！

钟韶琴，邓少林，刘昌厚敬上

韶琴
少林
昌厚

1997 年 12 月 1 日于新址
148 Flying Cloud Isle
Foster City, CA 94404
U.S.A.
Tel. (650)638-1917

China Beijing

中國北京

阜外大街北四巷 12 門 6 号

林瓊

U.S.A

148 Flying Cloud Isle

Foster City, CA 94404

Hen Tran Feng

中 国 建 筑 技 术 开 发 公 司

CHINA BUILDING TECHNIQUE DEVELOPMENT COMPANY

中国 北京   电话: 422.1354
                        电传: 210332 CABR CN
安外小黄庄路9号   电报: 北京 5912

钟大姐以及至德力克的儿媳：

敬祝您们新年快乐，万事如意！

您们分别给我们大家寄来的信和贺年片都收到了，谢谢，因为梦玉回去信封不好写，你让大家都不敢写，大家托我代写我也没有把握写好罢。

来信说，今年钟大姐动过两次大手术，我们一直也不知道，代写都能动手术？现在完全恢复了吗？存后您应该没有全心来信是，大姐报乐观，还主动于写信，并祝钟老年恒士，祝您成功！

您们寄加州的枣均香，这又可口，我们大家听了都说非常感谢。

下面向大姐汇报在京姐妹情况：年令最高 (8岁) 徐威尚大姐她，有一女三男，其中二个已退休了，一个是水利设计工作，一个是刊编辑，徐威尚大姐本人健康状况还好，徐维也今年86岁，姐部最后品应，头有一个眼睛看不到，发起信都听电话，她每次兄妹等三国聚计是当年堆党基本记（后毫政权），可是对超员作大情，现在是料材料公司面设，老三严本在储苗长教的，现已也生插公司。林瑞今年84岁身体还不多，有三男一女都在北京，老大程营奋工在见有成变，老二提型机械的主手如拍摘老三是的辑建筑工程，设计，还有量老少妻摄建材的产级销。

113

中国建筑技术开发公司
CHINA BUILDING TECHNIQUE DEVELOPMENT COMPANY

中国 北京

安外小黄庄路9号

电话：422.1954
电传：210332 CABR CN
电报：北京 5912

陈舜玉：今年83岁，她和林隆新（音）苹晶秉周，大学同学，也林瑞华一班，她现在也走了3次。她有3男3女，其中出家4个，外地2个。老大去清华大学念建筑报考一系，老二在南京，江沪大学教书，老三是女儿，北大毕业后留校工作，北也江沪江教书，老五、女，到科学二院，老六，在农学院，一班。

丁变今年80岁，她现在9小，她有2男3女，其中3个在家，2个到澳大利亚。在家的3个，一个在部队，一个在卫部，一个在建筑所。

胡瑞英79岁，她现也多小，她有4儿子在深圳劳公司任经理，4儿子在北京中共省部工作，一个儿子也已深圳，今儿也工留室教书（音）等，国务也几年辛苦时人才香上起了脑震荡手术。星珍今年75岁她有7个儿女，出家3个，外地4个，6个给给了3个，有的是研究员，音部工作，有的也科研工作。

以工厂人，寄去的照片中都有音，又有丁玉部（即陈沙中间圣睫替部份），将光的3部，它睫得拖本人也要音部二作

丁宁说她住部经络彩屏件寄去照片里是1支他都会给给寄电西寄信不方以放开寄，给待来邮回信，地也随看邮送回

现要去区川中珉沙是今年春季经过大炮，邀请我们这北京部区八大处旅游，它部里扑的唑，部爱丁宁没去，房以照片里没有她，祝全家欢乐，健康长寿！

徐召长的孙子、张纹凌，陈德庆，杜鹃，星珍，陈舜玉，丁变，胡瑞英，等

1998.12.19

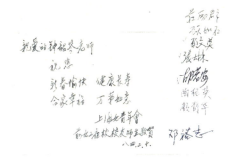

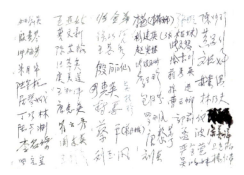

Figure 32 A New Year's Greeting Card sent on February 10, 1984. The signatures came from more than 64 former students and teachers of the Shanghai YWCA Night School. Among the signatures, there was one from Ms. Deng Yu-zhi (鄧裕志 or Cora Deng), former General Secretary of the China YWCA Association.

After the fall of the Gang of Four in 1976, former students and teachers of the Shanghai YWCA's Night School often gathered every couple of years. Among the old letters and photographs collected by mother, precious images were preserved:

- Group Photo (圖片 1): A snapshot capturing the camaraderie and shared memories of those who studied and/or taught in the night school. Faces filled with determination and hope, they stood together as a testament to their collective journey.

- Teacher and Students (圖片 2): In another photo, our mother, Helen Chung Teng (鍾韶琴), stood surrounded by her students and former colleagues. Their expressions reflected gratitude and respect. The bond between teacher and learners transcended time, echoing the impact of education on them

- Former Colleagues of Industrial Secretaries (圖片 26): Helen Chung Teng （1st from right）, Talitha Gerlach (耿麗淑, 2nd from right), Zhang Shu-yi (張淑義, 3rd from right).

These images evoke a sense of resilience, shared purpose, and the enduring legacy of education.

照片据原刊排名及当年的工的学校:

左一 里晓: 沪西女工夜校 特级班学生
左二 林琛: 〃 〃 〃 〃 老师
左三 陈舞玉: 〃 〃 〃 〃 〃
左四 王初: 浦东 〃 〃 老师
左五 孙丹凤: 〃 〃 〃 〃 〃
左六 陈继清: 沪西女工夜校·高级班老师
左七 胡瑞莱: 杨树浦女工夜校·学生

圖片 3 合影中左二是母親鍾韶琴（而不是林瓊）。

117

圖片 4 母親鍾韶琴（左三）和林瓊等女工夜校學生老師合影。

圖片 5 母親鍾韶琴女士（右一），耿麗淑（ Talitha Gerlach） 女士（右二），張淑義女士（右三）合影。

Appendix A Photos of Helen Chung Teng

Note: Very few lines of Chinese were translated into English in the following photos here to preserve the originality of Chinese names in their character format.

圖片 6 母親鍾韶琴（前排中），兒媳劉昌厚（前排左一），外孫許嶔（前排右一），兒子鄧少林（後排左一），小輩陳潔（後排右一）1996年聖誕期間在美國麻省 Acton 家中合影。

圖片 7 女兒鄧少筠和母親鍾韶琴女士在美國麻省 *Boxborough* 家中合影。

圖片 8 母親鍾韶琴參加兒子鄧少林 1987 年在美國麻省 WPI 碩士畢業典禮，了卻了父母教育子女的心願。

圖片 9 兒媳婦劉昌厚和母親鍾韶琴於 2003 年共度母親節。

圖片 10 母親鍾韶琴女士（後排左一），親家母岳闈娣女士（後排左二），親家許子慎先生（後排左三），女兒鄧少筠（前排左一），和外孫許嶔（左二）。女婿許維中在照相。

圖片 11　1977 年兒子女兒雙雙結婚。婚後合影：兒媳的外公周思敬（前排左一），外婆陳意（前排左二），母親鍾韶琴（前排左三），父親鄧衍林（前排左四），兒媳劉昌厚（後排左一），兒子鄧少林（後排左二），女婿許維中（後排左三），女兒鄧少筠（後排左四）。

圖片 12 2003 年 7 月家人為母親百歲過壽．前排：外孫許嶔（左一），女兒鄧少筠（左二），母親鍾韶琴（左三），親家母劉周紀穎（右二），

兒媳劉昌厚（右一）。後排：兒子鄧少林（右一），女婿許維中（左
一）。

圖片 13 1946 年攝於美國紐約。

圖片 14　1946 年左右攝於美國紐約。

圖片 15 1946 年左右攝於美國紐約。

圖片 16 1947 年攝於美國紐約。

圖片 17 一九五幾年父親鄧衍林，母親鍾韶琴在美國紐約。

圖片 18 1951 年左右攝於中國香港。

圖片 19 1951 年左右攝於中國香港。

圖片 20 1950 年左右攝於美國紐約。

圖片 21 1956 年 6 月攝於美國紐約。

圖片 22 二十世紀七十年代攝於北京。

圖片 23 攝於 1977 年左右。

Acknowledgement

Over the years, we have always wanted to publish a book about our mother. At last, we strived together and fulfilled this long-standing wish!

First, we would like to thank our cousin, Professor Zhong Shizhou (鍾世舟) of Zhong Shan University, Guang Zhou (中山大學，中國廣州), for encouraging us to pick up our pens and write about our memories of our mother. Our mother was Prof. Zhong's aunt. He provided a wealth of written and oral materials to the research paper on the Zhong's family by Tianjin Normal University. Prof. Zhong shared his stories about his father, Prof. Zhong Yuanzhao (鍾元昭), and his mother, Mrs. Kuang Jianlai (鄺健來), along with relevant background information about our mother.

Secondly, we express our greatest gratitude to our dear late Aunt Sally Biehusen[36] and Uncle/Major Henry Biehusen. Without their miracle actions, deep love, and generous financial help, Henry would not have made it back to the U.S. to start his college studies at Northeastern University, Boston at a very late stage of one's optimal learning curve. We like to thank our cousin David Chen and his family for their support to Henry in the 1980s and our cousin Jin Liang-juan (荊良娟), who made the arrangement for our father to get admitted into Beijing Hospital for his cancer treatment.

Thirdly, our thanks go to our older brother, Prof. Deng Yunsheng (鄧云生), for writing poems in memory of our fifth uncle, Zhong Hongjiu (鍾洪九), who was a fighter pilot (associated with the Flying Tiger squadron) in the anti-Japanese war in the 1940s. And we also like to thank our elementary school classmate, Mr. Zhang Qiying (張啓譽), who discovered and provided us with materials on our mother's 1956 registration form as a returning scholar to China.

In December 2018 and December 2023, the Institute for Ancient Book Preservation at Tianjin Normal University (天津师范大学古籍保护研究院) held commemorative events for our father's 110th and 115th birthday. We sincerely appreciate their efforts!

Finally, we wholeheartedly thank our dearest family members, wife Joan (Liu Chang-hou 劉昌厚) and husband Weizhong (許維中), for their unwavering love, help, and support in accomplishing this book of love of ours.

Henry S. Teng & Rosaline S. Teng Xu

鄧少林 & 鄧少苓

May 20, 2024

California, USA, and Beijing, China.

130

About the Authors

Henry S. Teng

Henry Shao-lin Teng (鄧少林) has been an early practitioner of Cybersecurity protection since the early 1980s. Henry started his security career in the Secure Systems Group of Digital Equipment Corporation (DEC), which was acquired by HP in 2002. He is a retired Certified Information Systems Security Professional (CISSP), former Certified Information Security Manager (CISM), and is the author and co-author of three U.S. patents[37] [38] [39] on artificial intelligence and its applications in the fields of computer security, network security, and application security. Henry has gained much of his security experience from working at several high-tech companies in Silicon Valley such as Charles Schwab Corporation, eBay Inc., KPMG LLP, and Royal Philips of The Netherlands.

Henry is a graduate of Northeastern University, Boston with summa cum laude and earned his Master of Science degree in Computer Science from Worcester Polytechnic Institute (WPI) in Massachusetts. He studied at the Graduate University of Chinese Academy of Sciences (GUCAS[40]).

Since retirement Henry has published about ten books[41] [42], continues to teach technology classes and/or offers webinars on Cybersecurity protection for non-profit organizations such as SCORE (www.score.org).

Rosaline S. Teng Xu

Rosaline S. Teng Xu was born in 1948 in New York City, USA. Her father's home town in China is Ji An City, Jiangxi Province (吉安市, 江西省). In 1976, Rosaline graduated from the Department of Radio Physics, Shanxi University (山西大學無綫電系) in China with a B.S. degree. In 1985, Rosaline completed her M.S. degree in Electrical Engineering from Worcester Polytechnic Institute (WPI) in Massachusetts. In the early 1980s, Rosaline began working for Digital Equipment Corporation in training for the installation and maintenance of large computer systems, including fault-tolerant computer systems and high-speed image workstations.

In 1997, Rosaline switched fields to health care products and returned to China to serve as the Chief Representative of the Yage International Entrepreneur Development Group. Her focuses shifted to adult continuing education, emphasizing three areas: financial education, happiness education, and health education. Rosaline serves dedicatedly as an advisor in cultivating family living qualities in the areas of comprehensive health, providing guidance on health management and planning, and researching how to improve quality of life, better aging, and promote longevity.

References

[1] Dr. Emily Honig, Professor Emerita of History at the University of California, Santa Cruz, Recruited as an undergraduate to join one of the first delegations of student leaders invited to visit China during the Cultural Revolution, she went on to complete an MA in East Asian Studies and a PhD in Chinese history at Stanford University. Dr. Emily Honig was a pioneering scholar whose research and teaching focused on modern China with particular attention to labor and gender.   1953 – 2023, https://www.legacy.com/us/obituaries/santacruzsentinel/name/emily-honig-obituary?id=53501884. For many years, the name of Emily Honig was not known despite Internet searches by the authors. Then a hint or clue came forward while reading Prof. Elizabeth A. Littell-lamb's book titled "The YWCA in China – The Making of a Chinese Christian Women's Institution, 1899 – 1957". The direct link between Dr. Honig and mother Helen Chung (or Zhong Shao-qin/鍾韶琴 in Pinyin) became evident when mother's name appeared in Dr. Honig's book titled "Sisters and Strangers: Women in the Shanghai Cotton Mills, 1919 – 1949".

[2] 王玉冰，《<钟氏家谱>的整理與研究》，天津師範大學研究生学位论文，文物與博物館学，古籍保护與传播專業，2022-05-25，第 24 頁："钟氏家族是书香门第，祖父鍾春晖 1880 年出生在福建古田县罗坑村。1904 年 24 崴的时候，毕业於英华中学，英文很好。之後便外出谋生，供职盐務三十余年，做过四川五通桥盐務所所长。钟春晖将政府所给的工资陆续汇到家中，在福州市南台区仓前山对湖购地建筑房屋，名曰"可园"。钟春晖为人老实正直，在四川任职时，主管的"五通桥"盐務所曾遭土匪抢劫，幸而损失很小，有人怂恿他向上级报告钱财已被土匪洗劫一空，可将钱财瓜分掉，遭到钟春晖的严词拒绝。"

[3] 中國人民政治协商会议第六届全國委员会名單

（https://baike.baidu.com/item/%E4%B8%AD%E5%9B%BD%E4%BA%BA%E6%B0%91%E6%94%BF%E6%B2%BB%E5%8D%8F%E5%95%86%E4%BC%9A%E8%AE%AE%E7%AC%AC%E5%85%AD

%E5%B1%8A%E5%85%A8%E5%9B%BD%E5%A7%94%E5%91%98%E4%BC%9A/6148570?fr=ala
ddin）。

4   民盟盟员担任第六届全國政协副主席、常務委员、委员名单（
https://www.mmzy.org.cn/mmgk/1191/11848.aspx）。

5   趙曉陽，《 20 世纪上半叶中國妇女的启蒙與觉醒 》，中華女子学院學報，（
Journal of China Women's University），2010 年 6 月第三期。
(https://ishare.iask.com.cn/f/19139778.html）。

6   Prof. Elizabeth A. Littell-Lamb, Women's History Review, 《Engendering a Class
Revolution: the Chinese YWCA industrial reform work in Shanghai, 1927–1939》,
p.205. (https://www.ut.edu/directory/littell-lamb-
elizabeth#:~:text=Her%20research%20focuses%20on%20the%20history%20of%20wome
n,in%20the%20cross-
cultural%20study%20of%20women%E2%80%99s%20social%20movements)。

7   趙曉陽,《 基督教会與劳工问题》，2007-05-16
（http://www.wyzxwk.com/Article/lishi/2009/09/15916.html。）

8   钟韶琴，上海市档案馆 U121-0-55-5，《我所看见的女工生活》1933 年 5 月
《女青年月刊》第 12 卷第 5 期 46 页）:"民國时期的上海，十幾崴进厂已经算大孩
子。更小的童工们 5-6 崴，7 崴以下的比比皆是。早上 3-4 点开工，到晚上 7 点或
更晚下班。中间 30 分钟吃饭，没有休息日。缲丝厂童工的工作是将茧投入沸水盆
搅动，再取出，刷去杂质，一天工作时间往往超过 10 小时，沸水溅出时常烫伤。
"手指因常與盆中沸水接触，致粗肿不忍卒者见。 "在棉纺厂的精纺、粗纺、弹
花、拆包等车间，工人需拆开原棉，扯松棉花，捡出杂质。空气中弥漫飞絮，不停
的钻进女童们的鼻孔、耳朵、眼睛、嘴巴里。"据调查每人平均要吸入 0.15 克花
絮"。上海工业医院成立於 1919 年，到 1923 年时，共救治纺织工人 880 名，其中
童工 150 人。从受伤部位来看，上肢 5%,下肢 30%,头部 15%,躯干 3%。其中因伤致
永久残废者占 29%,因伤致 死亡者占 3%。在纺织工厂中工作的童工身体瘦弱,形容
憔悴,多半含有结核性的病症。在英商怡和丝厂，女童工遭工头毒打的事件屡见不
鲜，有的被铜勺击伤头部,有的耳朵被扯伤,一个月之中,这类事件多至 15 至 20 起,

吓得有些童工不敢到厂上工。上海某袜厂一 12 岁左右童工，在一日当夜工时入睡，被管工的发现，就"把剪子一挥，戳那女童面上，鲜血淋漓"。尽管如此，还要流着血继续工作。"

9 Prof. Elizabeth A. Littell-Lamb, (https://www.ut.edu/directory/littell-lamb-elizabeth#:~:text=Her%20research%20focuses%20on%20the%20history%20of%20women,in%20the%20cross-cultural%20study%20of%20women%E2%80%99s%20social%20movements), Elizabeth A. Littell-Lamb is Associate Professor, History, University of Tampa, USA. She is the author of 'Localizing the Global: the YWCA movement in China, 1899 to 1939,' in Erika K. Kuhlman & Kimberly Jensen (Eds) Women and Transnational Activism in Historical Perspective (The Netherlands: Republic of Letters, 2010) and 'Gospel of the Body, Temple of the Nation: the YWCA movement and women's physical culture in China, 1915–1925,' in Research on Women in Modern Chinese History (Taiwan: Institute of Modern Chinese History, Academia Sinica, 2008). (https://www.tandfonline.com/doi/abs/10.1080/09612025.2012.657884?journalCode=rwhr20)

10 Elizabeth A. Littell-Lamb, 《Engendering a Class Revolution: The Chinese YWCA Industrial Reform Work in Shanghai 1927-1939》, 期刊 Women's History Review, Vol. 21, 2012 – Issue 2, p. 189-209.

(https://www.researchgate.net/publication/263568815_Engendering_a_Class_Revolution_the_Chinese_YWCA_industrial_reform_work_in_Shanghai_1927-1939); (https://www.tandfonline.com/doi/abs/10.1080/09612025.2012.657884?journalCode=rwhr20)

11 Sophia Smith Collection of Women's History, https://findingaids.smith.edu/repositories/2.

12 Yang Ai-fang, Chung Shou-ching (Helen Chung), Liu Yu-ying, May Bagwell, Sophia Smith Collection of Women's History, China YWCA Archive, smith_ssc_ms00324rg1_as90189_001-2024-04-11.pdf, p.75.

13 鍾韶琴，白美麗，劉媄, Sophia Smith Collection of Women's History, China YWCA Archive, smith_ssc_ms00324rg1_as90189_001-2024-04-11.pdf, p.74.

14 母親鍾韶琴女士參加女青年會夏令營的時間大約是 1930 年。

15 母親鍾韶琴女士根據附件她填寫的回國人員表格是滬江大學 1931 屆大學畢業。

16 趙曉陽，《基督教会與劳工问题》，"女青年会劳工工作随之开展起来。國內事務方面：女青年会继续依靠舆论发表文章、举办演讲，在社会上宣传中國近代工业情况，引起社会关注工业问题；努力與各地调查中國社会及经济机关合作，搞清情况，如长沙女青年会组织教师和学生，从事当地女工情况调查；烟台、天津女青年会进行女工调查；成都女青年会举行周日服務劳工界的活动；在大学里开设劳工课程，程婉珍曾任教於齐鲁大学，丁门任教於圣约翰大学；派干事单德馨[39]、袁荷莲、夏秀兰（Lily K. Haass）[40]到伦敦经济学院和美國学习研究劳工问题。1923 年秋，程婉珍到浙江等地访问了解劳工状况；1924 年至 1925 年，丁门到宁波、武汉等地考查劳动界状况，尤其注重童工的情况。各地任命了专职劳工干事办理事務，如袁荷莲、陶玲在烟台女青年会；邢德（E. Hinder）[41]、钱萃阁[42]、朱钰宝[43]、龚佩珍[44]、卢季卿[45]在上海女青年会劳工部；"

（http://www.wyzxwk.com/Article/lishi/2009/09/15916.html）

17 根據附件母親鍾韶琴女士填寫的回國人員表格，母親正式參加上海女青年會工作的時間是 1931 年。

18 May Bagwell, 'Industrial Work in Shanghai YWCA 1932,'April 1932, reel 51.2, YWCA Files, as a reference from 《Engendering a Class Revolution: the Chinese YWCA industrial reform work in Shanghai, 1927–1939》

(https://www.tandfonline.com/doi/full/10.1080/09612025.2012.657884?needAccess=true), Author Prof. Elizabeth Littell-Lamb (https://www.ut.edu/directory/littell-lamb-elizabeth。)

19 趙曉陽，《基督教会與劳工问题》，1930 年上海女青年会在小沙渡路三和里租了两幢房子（今西康路 910 弄 21－23 号），举办滬西女工社，楼下是女工夜校的课堂和课外活动场所，楼上是劳工部干事和教师的宿舍。上海女青年会劳工部干事钟韶琴和白美丽（M. Bagwell）一开始就迁入居住，1931 年下半年夏秀兰和邓裕志也先後迁入，30 年代後期劳工部干事耿丽淑（Talitha A. Gerlach）和张淑义都曾在三和里住过。(http://www.wyzxwk.com/Article/lishi/2009/09/15916.html。)

[20] 邓裕志(1900-1996)，女。湖北沙市人。全國妇联第一届常委，毕业於金陵女子大学社会学系。早年就积极投身於五四爱國运动，开办女工平民教育。在日本帝國主义入侵中國时，她和史良等妇女界领袖发起成立中國妇女救國会，1936 年又参與发起國难教育社，以推动抗日救亡运动的开展。建國後，邓裕志是中國基督教三自爱國运动的主要发起人之一，使中國基督教成为中國基督教徒自办的事业。

(https://baike.baidu.com/item/%E9%82%93%E8%A3%95%E5%BF%97?fromModule=lemma_search-box。)

[21] 母親鍾韶琴女士與上海女青年會的接觸始於女青年會的夏令營。

[22] 沈颖，《【人物春秋】妇幼干部张淑义》，"1936 年下半年，张淑义应聘到上海基督教女青年会任劳工部干事。当时上海抗日救國跃。女青年会总干事谢祖仪和劳工部主任干事钟韶琴都是爱國民主人士，经常参加各界、界的救國会活动。那时张淑义兼任女工夜校校长，主要任务是走访各厂区为筹办女工夜校舍；负责到租界地的工部局登记注册；选聘教师；请教师和文化界进步人士编写适合女工责辅导各校每周一次的"友光团"活动。"友光团"是号召"工友们团结起来，走上光明意，是女工夜校学生的自治组织。每次周会由学生自选代表主持，表演节目，在各班教师自编自演反映她们现实生活和革命要求的话剧，学演抗日歌曲、讲演、辩论等，活跃思想和创新的才能，用集体力量进行自我教育。"

[23] 华校生，《三和里女工夜校》，摘自《上海红色乡土故事选》： 抗战爆发后，女工夜校师生投入抗日洪流。滬西小沙渡路三和里(今西康路 910 弄 21-23 号) 是上海基督教女青年会开办的最有规模的一个女工夜校。刚从滬江大学毕业的钟韶琴到上海女青年会劳工部任干事，與邓裕志一起筹划在纱厂、丝厂、袜厂集中的滬西设立一个完全由女青年会自办的劳工服务处，熟悉女工状况，以求"教育和其他方法适应工人需求，并训练社会服务人才"。

[24] 张淑儀，《一二·九運動中的基督教學生 》，一九三六年下半年我到了上

139

海，參加基督教女青年會勞工部工作。當時上海抗日救國會已經很活躍，上海基督教女青年會總幹事謝祖儀和勞工部主任幹事鍾韶琴都是愛國民主人士，經常參加各界特別是婦女界的救國會活動。我初到那裏，主要任務是在各工廠區租借小學校的課堂，開辦女工識字學校。我負責選聘教師，請教師和文化界人士編寫適合女工需要的教材，還負責輔導各校每周一次的"友光團"活動。當時在上層知識婦女中成立勞工委員會。得到她們的支持贊助，在工廠區開辦了六個女工學校，有一千二百左右的女工學生，近三十名教師。高級班和特級班的教材有大眾哲學，社會發展史、簡單的革命史等。當時提倡"小先生制"，有些教師就由本校畢業的女工學生擔任，有些是進步朋友和婦救會推薦的革命知識分子如羅曉紅(解放後曾任全國婦聯主席蔡暢的秘書)、胡瑞英(曾任江西省總工會副主席)、陳維清(曾任紡織工業部顧問)等；女工出身的教師如李淑英(曾任食品工業工會主席，全國政協委員)、盧英(曾任撫順市女市長)，任秀棠(已故，曾任廣州市出口商品檢驗局副局長)等。女工學校學生的自治組織"友光團"是工友們團結起來走向光明大道之意。每次周會由學生自己主持，表演節目，反映她們的生活現實和革命要求，學唱抗日歌曲，表演話劇，演講辯論等，鍛煉她們的口才，活躍思想，用集體力量進行自我教育。教師和千事共同輔導，并請當時的教育家陶行知去演講，進步音樂家如孟波、麥新教唱救亡歌曲，導演崔嵬指導她們演劇。女工自己編的歌劇《我們爲啥生活這樣苦》，描述日本紗廠女工受壓迫受剝削的情況和覺醒，還有《女性歌》，她們深有體會，演唱起來十分感人，使大家受到教育。她們由不識字到識字，文化、政治水平不斷提高，革命意志更加堅強。各校女工學生踴躍參加曆次罷工鬥爭、抗日救亡遊行示威等活動。"八·一三"抗戰在上海爆發後，她們先後組織兩個"勞動婦女戰地服務團"到内地參加抗戰，爲傷兵服務。有的參加新四軍，有的到延安進抗大、女大、魯藝學習。解放後，許多曾在女工學校讀書的人，飽經考驗，成爲革命幹部，在各條戰線發揮重要作用。

（https://www.krzzjn.com/show-1244-62260.html。）

[25] 高參 88， 西康路 902 弄三和里 21-23 号是 1930 年至 1949 年上海基督教女青年会女工夜校旧址。

1929 年底，面对社会劳资纠纷日增的局面，女青年会全国协会拨专款支持，與上海女青年会劳工部共同计划，在女工集中的地方设立一个完全由女青年会自办的劳工服务处，作为女青年会劳工工作的示范点，以便在全國推广。1930 年，女青年会全國协会劳工部干事邓裕志和上海女青年会劳工部干事钟绍琴，在小沙渡路三和里（今西康路 902 弄 21-23 号）租下两幢房，办起了女工夜校。因为地处三和里，所以称三和里女工夜校。楼下是教室和课外活动场地，楼上是教师宿舍。

(http://www.360doc.com/content/22/0221/22/11742065_1018444822.shtml。)

[26] 钟韶琴，上海市档案馆 U121-0-55-5，《我所看见的女工生活》1933 年 5 月《女青年月刊》第 12 卷第 5 期 46 页）:"民國时期的上海，十幾崴进厂已经算大孩子。更小的童工们 5-6 崴，7 岁以下的比比皆是。早上 3-4 点开工，到晚上 7 点或更晚下班。中间 30 分钟吃饭，没有休息日。繰丝厂童工的工作是将茧投入沸水盆搅动，再取出，刷去杂质，一天工作时间往往超过 10 小时，沸水溅出时常烫伤。"手指因常與盆中沸水接触，致粗肿不忍卒者见。"在棉纺厂的精纺、粗纺、弹花、拆包等车间，工人需拆开原棉，扯松棉花，捡出杂质。空气中弥漫飞絮，不停的钻进女童们的鼻孔、耳朵、眼睛、嘴巴里。"据调查每人平均要吸入 0.15 克花絮"。上海工业医院成立於 1919 年，到 1923 年时，共救治纺织工人 880 名，其中童工 150 人。从受伤部位来看，上肢 5%,下肢 30%,头部 15%,躯干 3%。其中因伤致永久残废者占 29%,因伤致 死亡者占 3%。在纺织工厂中工作的童工身体瘦弱，形容憔悴,多半含有结核性的病症。在英商怡和丝厂，女童工遭工头毒打的事件屡见不鲜，有的被铜勺击伤头部,有的耳朵被扯伤,一个月之中,这类事件多至 15 至 20 起，吓得有些童工不敢到厂上工。上海某袜厂一 12 崴左右童工，在一日当夜工时入睡，被管工的发现，就"把剪子一挥，截那女童面上，鲜血淋漓"。尽管如此，还要流着血继续工作。"

[27] 上海勞動婦女抗日戰地服務團首批成员有 10 人，她們是: 任秀堂(22 歲、12 歲當童工)、胡瑞英（22 歲、8 歲當童工）、鄭慧珍（20 歲）、李亞芬（16 歲、12 歲當童工）、金敏玉（16 歲、15 歲當童工）、李惠英（22 歲、12 歲當童工）、張定堡（17 歲）、龔琦瑋（17 歲）、秦秋谷（20 歲）、柳秀娟（23 歲）。

(https://kknews.cc/history/59gvq96.html。)

[28] 胡蘭畦（1901 年 6 月 22 日 - 1994 年 12 月 13 日），出生於四川成都。她是中

國的作家和軍事將領。1927 年，畢業於武汉黄埔軍校女生隊。1929 年，赴德國留学。1930 年，經廖承志和成仿吾介紹，加入中國共产党，编入德國共产党中國语言组 1939 年夏 蒋介石委任胡兰畦為國民政府軍事委員會战地党政委員会少将指导員，前往第三、六、九戰區。

https://zh.wikipedia.org/zh/%E8%83%A1%E5%85%B0%E7%95%A6。

29 陈宏玮,＜【红色记忆】11 支铿锵玫瑰上海劳动妇女战地服务团>, 2021-12-13 04:49, https://mp.weixin.qq.com, "江西 1937 年 9 月，胡兰畦到上海基督教女青年会女工夜校做报告，了解到夜校女工学员爱國热情高，能吃苦耐劳，就请夜校钟韶琴校长帮助组织队伍。在当时，夜校学生、共青团江苏临时省委组织部长胡瑞英听到这一消息，立刻向临时团省委书记陈國栋报告了情况，并马上去夜校找老师，坚决要求参加服务团，并协助老师挑选人员。服务团最後确定了包括 9 名女工学员及 1 名夜校老师在内的 10 名成员（任秀棠、胡瑞英、李亚芬、金敏玉、郑惠珍、李惠英、张定堡、龚琦玮、秦秀谷、柳秀娟）。因服务团以女工为主，故起名为上海劳动妇女战地服务团。胡兰畦任团长。

30 蔡鸿源，徐友春，《 民國会社党派大辞典 》黄山书社，2012.08，第 44 页："云南基督教女青年会是 1938 年在云南昆明成立的社会团体，以"本基督之精神，促进妇女德、智、体、群、美育之发展"为宗旨。该会设董事会，会长为缪云台夫人，总干事为钟韶琴，学生部干事为李鉴，总务干事为刘有庆，成人部干事为常绍美，宿舍部干事为余兰英，抗属福利部为刘永兰乏，第二宿舍部干事为余华英。会址设在云南昆明南屏街。"

（https://baike.baidu.com/item/%E4%BA%91%E5%8D%97%E5%9F%BA%E7%9D%A3%E6%95%99%E5%A5%B3%E9%9D%92%E5%B9%B4%E4%BC%9A/23189195?fr=Aladdin。）

31 张淑义，女。直隶（今河北）三河人。1935 年加入中國共产党。次年毕业於燕京大学社会学系。1943 年获美國哥伦比亚大学社会工作学院社会科学硕士学位。曾任上海基督教女青年会劳工部主任、中华基督教女青年会全國协会劳工兼民众教育部干事、平山县洛杉矶托儿所秘书。建國後，历任全國妇联國际联络部副部长、中國人民保卫儿童全國委員会秘书长、全國妇联第四届执委、中國联合國协会理事、欧美同学会副会长。是第四、五届全國政协委員。

（https://baike.baidu.com/item/%E5%BC%A0%E6%B7%91%E4%B9%89/5786447?fr=alad din）

32 周余嬌，《中國图书馆学报》2017 年第 1 期。

（http://www.sohu.com/a/272099297_717218）

33 趙曉陽，"基督教会與劳工问题"，中國社会科学院近代史研究所 網聯：

http://jds.cass.cn/ztyj/shwhs/201605/t20160506_3325937.shtml

34 US Patent US5812763A, Teng, Henry Shao-Lin, "Expert system having a plurality of security inspectors for detecting security flaws in a computer system", issued 1998-09-22. (https://patents.google.com/patent/US5812763A/en?oq=US5812763A);

US Patent US5222197A, Teng, Henry S.; Chen, Kaihu & Wilson, Matthew et al., "Rule invocation mechanism for inductive learning engine", issued 1993-06-22.

(https://patents.google.com/patent/US5222197A/en?oq=US5222197A);

US Patent US5034898A, Lu, Stephen C-Y; Teng, Henry S.; Tseng, Mitch et al., "System including inductive learning arrangement for adaptive management of behavior of complex entity", issued 1991-07-23.

(https://patents.google.com/patent/US5034898A/en?q=(teng)&inventor=henry+s&oq= henry+s+teng)

35 《Journey in Volunteering over Two Decades (公益助人幾十年的歷程)》，作者 Henry S. Teng (鄧少林)，全書共 322 頁， ISBN 9798800820188， ISBN 9798884995680， ISBN 9798321009116 (Hardcover)， Amazon Kindle Direct Publishing U.S.A. (美國亞馬遜書局出版)， 2022 年出版。

36 Sally Biehusen, https://www.legacy.com/us/obituaries/palmbeachpost/name/sally-biehusen-crum-obituary?id=27219308

37 US Patent US5034898A, Lu, Stephen C-Y; Teng, Henry S.; Tseng, Mitch et al., "System including inductive learning arrangement for adaptive management of behavior of complex entity", issued 1991-07-23.

(https://patents.google.com/patent/US5034898A/en?q=(teng)&inventor=henry+s&oq= henry+s+teng)

[38] US Patent US5222197A, Teng, Henry S.; Chen, Kaihu & Wilson, Matthew et al., "Rule invocation mechanism for inductive learning engine", issued 1993-06-22. (https://patents.google.com/patent/US5222197A/en?oq=US5222197A)

[39] US Patent US5812763A, Teng, Henry Shao-Lin, "Expert system having a plurality of security inspectors for detecting security flaws in a computer system", issued 1998-09-22. (https://patents.google.com/patent/US5812763A/en?oq=US5812763A)

[40] University of Chinese Academy of Sciences was established with the approval of Ministry of Education of the People's Republic of China (PRC). Its predecessor, Graduate University of Chinese Academy of Sciences (GUCAS), was the first graduate school in China. https://english.ucas.ac.cn/

[41] 《Journey in Volunteering over Two Decades 》, Henry S. Teng, 322 pages, ISBN 9798800820188, ISBN 9798884995680, ISBN 9798321009116 (Hardcover), Amazon Kindle Direct Publishing U.S.A., 2022.

[42] 《Artificial Intelligence Towards Cybersecurity Protection - A Representative Collection of Early Research Work and Practice 》, Henry S. Teng, 253 pages, ISBN 9781713292753, ISBN 9798883496126, ISBN 9798321422113 （Hardcover）, Amazon Kindle Direct Publishing U.S.A., 2020.

Made in the USA
Monee, IL
06 July 2024

7a4d8ed6-5aa0-46c9-921f-eeeca7d63c89R02